The Judges Testify of

CHRIST

&

Give us

HOPE

God's faithfulness to His Word and His People

RUSSELL H. KENT

Copyright © 2014 by Russell H. Kent

The Judges Testify of Christ and Give us Hope
God's faithfulness to His Word and His People
by Russell H. Kent

Printed in the United States of America

ISBN 9781629524405

All rights reserved solely by the author. The author guarantees all contents are original and do not infringe upon the legal rights of any other person or work. No part of this book may be reproduced in any form without the permission of the author. The views expressed in this book are not necessarily those of the publisher.

Unless otherwise indicated, Bible quotations are taken from the New King James Version. Copyright 1979, 1980, 1982 by Thomas Nelson, Inc. Used by permission. All rights reserved.

To My Wife
Who for forty years
has been
lover, companion, and partner
by the Grace of God.

TABLE OF CONTENTS

David & Linda:

May the Lord bless you and grant you peace. May you bless others in the name of our King.

Russell M. Nelson

ACKNOWLEDGMENTS

I would like to acknowledge the following people for their invaluable contributions to the making of this book:

My wife, Jean, who unflaggingly encouraged me throughout the years.

My children who have encouraged me to write and be published.

Dr. Carl Armerding, my professor at Regent College (1984–1988), who encouraged me to turn my Th.M. thesis into a book.

Lenard Seeley, a rancher in Wyoming, who used my material to teach others and has encouraged me to be published.

Phil Taggart, friend of fifty plus years who has encouraged me through many "dark hours" and wrestled with me as we plumbed the depths of faith.

Dr. Larry Keefauver, my editor, who made many invaluable suggestions and encouraged me to be me.

David Green, fellow member of the New England Reformed Fellowship, who freely shared with me his thoughts on the failure of the Priests during the Era of the Judges.

Various people throughout: Wyoming, Mississippi, Washington, Illinois, and Massachusetts who have used my material and been encouraged, stretched, and edified by it. All of these people were brought into my life by the Sovereign Covenant God who has redeemed me from the pit. My prayer is that this book redound to His Glory and is used by Him to edify and encourage His Church.

Introduction

LEARN OF JESUS AND HAVE HOPE

And they said to one another, "Did not our heart burn within us while He talked with us on the road, and while He [Jesus the risen Christ] opened the Scriptures to us?" (Luke 24:32)

W hy study the Old Testament? The study of the Old Testament can be motivated by a number of interests—to study the history of Israel, to learn of the religion of the Jews, etc. While personal reasons may motivate some curiosity about the Old Testament, according to the witness of the New Testament, there are two predominant reasons to study the Old Testament: *to learn of Jesus and to have hope.*

As He spoke to the Jews, Jesus identified four witnesses that bore testimony of His person and character:

- John the Baptist,
- Jesus' own work,
- the Father who sent Him,
- and the Scriptures.[1]

Jesus tells the Jews that Moses is their accuser, for if they had believed Moses they would have believed Jesus. According to Jesus, Moses wrote of Jesus the Christ (Messiah). When Jesus speaks of the writings of Moses, He is speaking of the Torah: Genesis, Exodus, Leviticus, Numbers, and Deuteronomy. Jesus includes the whole of the Old Testament as speaking of Him as He walks on the road to Emmaus.[2] Luke tells us that Jesus began with Moses and explained to the two disciples the things that concerned Him in all the Scriptures.

In Luke 24, Jesus appears to the disciples saying to them, "These are the words which I spoke to you while I was still with you, that all things must be fulfilled which were written in the Law of Moses and the Prophets and the Psalms concerning Me." Luke continues to write that Jesus opened their minds to the Scriptures.[3] Therefore, as we study the Old Testament, we ought to "seek Jesus" and learn how God has revealed His Son within the pages of the Old Testament.

Paul, writing to the Church at Rome, asserts, "For whatever things were written before were written for our learning, that we through the patience and comfort of the Scriptures might have hope."[4] Earlier in the Book of Romans referring to the promise Yahweh made to Abram in Genesis 15, Paul instructs, "Now it was not written for his sake alone that it was imputed to him, but also for us."[5] Therefore as we think about the Old Testament, we can be encouraged as we learn how God has worked among humanity. This learning process will result in hope for ourselves in whatever circumstances we find ourselves

As we study the Old Testament, we ought to "seek Jesus" and learn how God has revealed His Son within the pages of the Old Testament.

So, why study the Old Testament, especially the book of Judges? It appears on the surface to be an ancient, even archaic, collection of stories about an obscure people trying to survive in a new homeland. However, buried within these stories are nuggets of revelation about Christ that will strengthen our faith, comfort our hearts, and bring healing to our hurts. Therefore, this book is intended to help us discover how Judges testifies of Jesus, the Christ, and to determine how we may be comforted with hope as a result of the things we learn from Judges.

Furthermore, knowing that the Christ in you is the hope of glory will transform your life:

1. *from discouragement to courage;*
2. *from despair to expectation;*
3. *from shame to glory;*
4. *and from impotence and inferiority to power and overcoming confidence.*

I am inviting you to be surprised by how God is speaking to your life, particularly your difficulties, trials, and pain, through this book of Judges—filled with revelation, wisdom, and insight for your life. The Great Physician, Jesus Christ, will meet you in these ancient texts with amazing truths about your life in the 21ˢᵗ century. Be encouraged as you read these pages in hope and expectation!

Chapter 1

INQUIRING OF YAHWEH

Ready for a great, true story? A seminary professor, Dr. Fred Craddock, was vacationing with his wife in Gatlinburg, TN. One morning, they were eating breakfast at a little restaurant, hoping to enjoy a quiet family meal. While they were waiting for their food, they noticed a distinguished looking, white-haired man moving from table to table, visiting with the guests.

The professor leaned over and whispered to his wife, "I hope he doesn't come over here."

But sure enough, the man did come over to their table.

"Where are you folks from?" he asked in a friendly voice.

"Oklahoma," they answered.

"Great to have you here in Tennessee," the stranger said. "What do you do for a living?"

"I teach at a seminary," Professor Craddock replied.

"Oh, so you teach preachers how to preach, do you? Well, I've got a really great story for you," the gentleman said as he pulled up a chair and sat down at the table with the couple.

The professor groaned and thought to himself, "Great. Just what I need, another preacher story!"

The man started, "See that mountain over there? (pointing out the restaurant window). Not far from the base of that mountain, there was a boy born to an unwed mother. He had a hard time growing up because every place he went he was always asked the same question, 'Hey boy, Who's your daddy?' Whether he was at school, in the grocery store or drug store people would ask the same question."

"This boy would hide at recess and lunch from other students. He would avoid going into stores because that question hurt him so bad," the gentleman continued. "When he was about twelve years old, a new preacher came to his church. He would always go in late and slip out early to avoid hearing the question, 'Who's your daddy?' But one day, the new preacher said the benediction so fast that the boy got trapped and had to walk out with the crowd. Just about the time he got to the back door, the new preacher, not knowing anything about him, put his hand on his shoulder and asked him, 'Son, who's your daddy?' The whole church got deathly quiet. He could feel every eye in the church looking at him. Now everyone would finally know the answer to the question."

With a twinkle in his eye, the gentleman said, "This new preacher sensed the situation around him and using discernment that only the Holy Spirit could give, said to that scared little boy, 'Wait a minute! I know who you are! I see the family resemblance now. *You are a child of God.*' With that he patted the boy on his shoulder and added, 'Boy, you've got a great inheritance. Go and claim it.'"

"With that, the boy smiled for the first time in a long time and walked out the door a changed person. He was never the same again. Whenever anybody asked him, 'Who's your Daddy?' he'd just tell them, 'I'm a Child of God.'"

The distinguished gentleman got up from the table and said, "Isn't that a great story?"

The professor responded that it really was a great story!

As the man turned to leave he said, "You know, if that new preacher hadn't told me that I was one of God's children, I probably never would have amounted to anything!" And he walked away.

The seminary professor and his wife were stunned. He called the waitress over and asked her, "Do you know who that man was, the one who just left that was sitting at our table?"

The waitress grinned and said, "Of course. Everybody here knows him. That's Ben Hooper. He's governor of Tennessee!"[6]

The awesome God of Mt. Sinai, Yahweh, desires a covenant relationship with you as your Father. Did you know that you are included in God's covenant promises to Abraham, Moses, the Judges, and the Old Testament prophets? The blessing on Abraham's life is for you. Maybe you have felt like that little boy who didn't know his father. Perhaps you have found yourself recently experiencing more failures than successes, more hurt than healing or more curses than blessings. There may be a family member, a friend or even a church member who has attacked you, abused you or demeaned you. In life we discover that relationships are everything, and they can be filled with injury and insult more often than not, especially with those closest to us. Yet from the earliest pages of the Old Testament, we learn that the God of the Universe, the Eternal *I Am* (Yahweh), desires a personal, intimate, close relationship with each of us. His will is to bless us not curse us; to save us not condemn us; and to lift us up not beat us down. This is a truth that the judges discovered. Let's discover what they uncovered about God that can transform our lives with the knowledge of the hope that God is with us—we are blessed and not alone.

The Book of Judges begins with a leadership void. Israel felt abandoned and alone. Their prophetic leader out of Egypt and through the Wilderness, Moses, had died. Joshua, the one whom had been appointed by Yahweh (the "I am that I am" name of God revealed to Moses in Exodus 3) to lead the Sons of Israel as Moses' successor, had also died. Joshua had inquired of Yahweh by standing before the priest who would inquire of Yahweh by means of Urim (Numbers 27:15-23). When Joshua and the men of Israel failed to seek the counsel of Yahweh, they were duped into making a covenant with the Gibeonites, a people they were to have driven out of Canaan.[7]

It can be assumed that the Sons of Israel continued to inquire of Yahweh through the priest using Urim and Thummin in Judges 1:1. That the Sons of Israel inquired of Yahweh assumes a relationship that underlies the whole of the Book of Judges. This relationship was / is rooted in the Abrahamic Covenant from Genesis 12:1-3.

> *Get out of your country, From your family And from your father's house, To a land that I will show you. I will make you a great nation; I will bless you and make your name great; and you shall be a blessing. I will bless those who bless you, and I will curse him who curses you; and in you all the families of the earth shall be blessed.*

Later in Genesis 15:1, Yahweh speaks to Abram saying, "I am your shield, your exceedingly great reward." Yahweh gives Himself to Abram thus obligating Himself to serve Abram. Yahweh promises Abram an heir and descendants as numerous as the stars, further obligating Himself. Abram believes the word of Yahweh and is reckoned righteous. On that day Yahweh makes a covenant with Abram.[8] Yahweh, again commits to Abraham (name changed in Genesis 17: 5) in Genesis 17 and 22. In Genesis 22 Yahweh swears by Himself as the covenant with Abraham is reiterated. The Covenant with Abraham is passed on to Isaac and Jacob.

As the Sons of Israel languished as slaves in Egypt they groaned. God heard their groaning, and God remembered His covenant with Abraham, with Isaac, and with Jacob. God looked upon the children of Israel and acknowledged them. God meets Moses in the wilderness at Horeb, the mountain of God. God identifies Himself as "...the God of Abraham, the God of Isaac, and the God of Jacob." God tells Moses that He has seen the affliction of the Sons of Israel and has come to deliver them from Egypt and lead them to a land "flowing with milk and honey."[9] God then commissions Moses to be the one to lead Israel out of Egypt. It is during the commissioning of Moses that God reveals the significance of His name Yahweh. Moses is told that Yahweh was the God of the patriarchs and that Yahweh was to be His name forever, a "memorial-name to all generations."[10] This name is to be the Covenantal name signifying the relationship and obligations incurred by God with respect to His people.

The relationship rooted in the Abrahamic Covenant is further defined by the Covenant made at Sinai. Israel, having been delivered from bondage, is given a vocation. God declared that Israel was to be a "... special treasure to Me above all people; for all the earth is Mine. And you shall be to Me a kingdom of priests and a holy nation."[11] How this vocation is to be fulfilled is the subject matter of Exodus, Leviticus, Numbers, and Deuteronomy. But the vocation is succinctly summarized in the Decalogue in Exodus 20:3-17. The Decalogue is introduced with these words, "I am the LORD your God, who brought you out of the land of Egypt, out of the house of bondage." With these words the act of deliverance is placed within the Abrahamic Covenant. The deliverance from Egypt and the house of bondage was the result of Yahweh's promise to Abraham. Therefore the Law that follows does not define how to have a relationship with Yahweh but is descriptive of the vocation given to Israel as a result of being the "People of Yahweh." The relationship between Yahweh and the Sons of Israel may be understood as the relationship between a king and his vassal.

A treaty or covenant between a king and his vassal was a treaty made between a greater and a lesser. Such a treaty/covenant was drawn up between two parties who already had established a relationship whereby the lesser was dependent on the greater. In such a treaty the king promised to provide the vassal with certain benefits such as defense, provisions, and a just government. The vassal in return promised loyalty and faithful allegiance to the king. The treaty/covenant usually included consequences if the covenant was broken. The treaty was also witnessed by the "gods" of the king and the vassal. The Sinaitic Covenant is a covenant made between the Great King, Yahweh and His Vassal the Sons of Israel. Just as a foretaste of what's coming, I want you to know that Yahweh's son, Jesus the Messiah, takes that Israelite covenant and expands it into a New Covenant including you in it! More about that later in this book.

> **Just as a foretaste of what's coming, I want you to know that Yahweh's son, Jesus the Messiah, takes that Israelite covenant and expands it into a New Covenant including you in it!**

The whole of the Old Testament attests to the unique character of Yahweh. Not only is He the God of Israel, but He is also superior to the gods of all nations.[12] Yahweh is the Great King over all the Earth.[13] Yahweh is the Creator,[14] and Deliverer.[15] Yahweh, the great King, enters into a Covenantal relationship with the Sons of Israel. Exodus 20-24 provides the information that defines the nature of this Covenant.

Yahweh had brought the Sons of Israel out of Egypt and in three months had led them to the mountain. Here Yahweh gives Israel laws that define how the Israelites are to demonstrate that they are Yahweh's peculiar people. The Covenant was ratified by the people as they said, "All the words which Yahweh has said we will do." Moses wrote down all that Yahweh had said. An altar was built and burnt offerings and peace offerings were made to Yahweh. Blood was sprinkled on the altar; the book of the covenant was read. The people again said, "All that the LORD has said we will do, and be obedient." Moses then sprinkled blood upon the people saying, "This is the blood of the covenant which the LORD has made with you according to all these words." Following this ratification of the Covenant, Moses, Aaron, Nadab, Abihu, and seventy elders of Israel ascended the mountain where they saw God and ate and drank. The Sinaitic Covenant establishes Yahweh as King in Israel.

Jesus Fulfills the Abrahamic and Sinaitic Covenants

The Abrahamic Covenant and the Sinaitic Covenant not only underlie the Book of Judges, they also underlie the rest of the Old Testament as well as the New Testament. Both Covenants are fulfilled in the person of Jesus, the Christ. Mary, as she exalts in the Lord, reiterating what God has done, closes with, "He has helped His servant Israel, In remembrance of His mercy, As He spoke to our fathers, To Abraham and to his seed forever." Zacharias says that which God is doing is, "To perform the mercy promised to our fathers and to remember His holy covenant, The oath which He swore to our father Abraham...." Paul, in Galatians, specifically identifies Jesus, the Christ, as the seed of Abraham in the promise given in Genesis 22.

As God's child by faith in Jesus, you are included in the Abrahamic Covenant. In Jesus you are also reckoned to be righteous for Jesus has fulfilled the Law for you and borne the penalty of the Law for you.

Jesus came to fulfill the Sinaitic Covenant for as He said: "Do not think that I came to destroy the Law or the Prophets. I did not come to destroy but to fulfill. For assuredly, I say to you, till heaven and earth pass away, one jot or one tittle will by no means pass from the law till all is fulfilled."[16]

Jesus summarized the Sinaitic Covenant by quoting from Deuteronomy and Leviticus saying:

"'You shall love the LORD your God with all your heart, with all your soul, and with all your mind.' This is the first and great commandment. And the second is like it: 'You shall love your neighbor as yourself.' On these two commandments hang all the Law and the Prophets."[17]

Not only are the Abrahamic Covenant and the Sinaitic Covenant fulfilled by Jesus, but the Covenantal name Yahweh and all that it signifies is borne by Jesus for the name Jesus means Yahweh Saves. Therefore Jesus was / is Immanuel, God with us.

Therefore, dear reader, as God's child by faith in Jesus, you are included in the Abrahamic Covenant. In Jesus you are also reckoned to be righteous, for Jesus has fulfilled the Law for you and borne the penalty of the Law for you. Thus in Christ, you fulfill the obligations of the Sinaitic Covenant. Being included in the Abrahamic Covenant and having fulfilled the Sinaitic Covenant through Christ, you now have a vocation: you "... are a chosen generation, a royal priesthood, a holy nation, His own special people, that you may proclaim the praises of Him who called you out of darkness into His marvelous light; who once were not a people but are now the people of God, who had not obtained mercy but now have obtained mercy."[18]

In 1938...I was suffering from splitting headaches; each sound hurt me like a blow.... I discovered the poem...called "Love" [by George Herbert] which I learnt by heart. Often, at the culminating point of a violent headache, I made myself say it over, concentrating all my attention upon it and clinging with all my soul to the tenderness it enshrines. I used to think I was merely reciting it as a beautiful poem, but without my knowing it the recitation had the virtue of a prayer. It was during one of these recitations that Christ himself came down and took possession of me. In my arguments about the insolubility of the problem of God I had never foreseen the possibility of that, of a real contact, person to person, here below, between a human being and God.

   ■ Simone Weil, Waiting for God

Yahweh, the Living God, wants real contact with us—a covenant relationship with us through the risen Christ. Within His new covenant, we find our identity in Christ as priests and kings. We understand that His ministry as Priest, Prophet, and King has been imbedded in us. We know what was discovered by a young boy without an earthly father, "I'm a child of God."

Ask Yourself...

- *When did I learn that I was a child of God? How has that changed my life?*
- *If I'm living a lonely, abandoned, and orphaned life, when God desires for me to live as a chosen and royal child, then what do I need to do to live like my Daddy's child?*

- *Whenever I focus on the dark side of my circumstances, difficulties, trials, and hurts, what can I do to revive my hope, blessings, and God's promises for my life?*

Here are some action steps you can begin with today. Check them off as you complete them.

- Read every passage quoted and listed in this chapter and commit it to memory for your spiritual growth.
- Focus on a relationship in your life that makes you feel abandoned, orphaned, or abused. Confess your hurt and pain to Christ. Decide to forgive. Release the past. Begin thinking and acting like a child of God, a new creation in Christ. (Read and live out Galatians 5.)
- Make a life of people you know who are ignorant of or have forgotten the blessings of being in a covenant relationship with Yahweh. Pray for them daily. When God tells you how to reach out to them, decide to obey Him.
- What is God telling you to do right now after reading this chapter? Write it down.

Chapter 2

COVENANT BREACH AND RENEWAL

A s the pastor of a small community church on the Western Plains I was asked to perform many marriages. As I had been counseled by my various mentors, I always requested those wishing to be married to come for a series of premarital counseling sessions. This one couple came from a community at least fifty miles away for one of their counseling sessions. The session went something like this:

"Good afternoon Lester. Good afternoon Pricilla. Please sit down. Before we begin let us ask the Lord for wisdom as we seek His will for your lives."

We then prayed. Following the prayer, I gave each of them a Bible and asked them to turn to Ephesians 5, and we read the passage that defines marriage as a model of Christ and the Church.

I asked Lester, "Do you understand that you are to love Pricilla as Jesus loves the Church? Do you understand that you are entering into a covenant relationship? Do you know what that means?"

Lester leaned forward, elbows on the table and chin in hands, and said "I know what I read, but not what it means."

I then spoke to Lester of the life, death, and resurrection of Jesus. I spoke of how Jesus lived for us in active obedience. I spoke of how Jesus died for us in passive obedience. I then said that Jesus' love for the church was the model for his love for Pricilla.

I asked Lester, "Are you prepared to live and, if necessary, die for Pricilla?"

Lester was quite still and silent for a spell. I glanced at Pricilla. It was obvious she liked what she heard. She wanted to be loved with a love that was totally focused on her welfare.

Lester finally said, "I love Pricilla and will enter into such a covenant."

I then turned to Pricilla and asked her if she wanted a husband who would love her as Jesus loved the Church. She was quite enthusiastic with her affirmative answer.

I then said, "Pricilla, are you willing to submit to Lester as the Church submits to Jesus? Do you understand what that means?"

Pricilla wasn't certain she understood, so I began to explain it to her. The more I talked the more agitated she became until she pushed her chair back, got up, and stormed out of the room. Lester's jaw dropped as he became very still.

"Pastor, what do I do now?" he asked.

"It is up to you, Lester," I told him. "Do you love her? If you love her, what is required?"

Lester slowly rose to his feet and walked out.

This covenant relationship required both love and obedience. Israel was confronted with such a covenant in the Wilderness. The Sons of Israel were promised great blessing if they kept the covenant as they said that they would do at the base of Sinai. The Covenant and the promise of blessing on the condition of obedience are summarized in Deuteronomy 30:9-16.

> *Yahweh your God will make you abound in all the work of your hand, in the fruit of your body, in the increase of your livestock, and in the produce of your land for good. For Yahweh will again rejoice over you for good as He rejoiced over your fathers, if you obey the voice of Yahweh your God, to keep His commandments and His statutes which are written in this Book of the Law, and if you turn to Yahweh your God with all your heart and with all your soul. For this commandment which I command you today is not too mysterious for you, nor is it far off. It is not in heaven, that you should say, "Who will ascend into heaven for us and bring it to us, that we may hear it and do it?" Nor is it beyond*

> *the sea, that you should say, "Who will go over the sea for us and bring it to us, that we may hear it and do it?" But the word is very near you, in your mouth and in your heart, that you may do it. See, I have set before you today life and good, death and evil, in that I command you today to love Yahweh your God, to walk in His ways, and to keep His commandments, His statutes, and His judgments, that you may live and multiply; and Yahweh your God will bless you in the land which you go to possess.*

But if the Sons of Israel broke the Covenant, there would not be blessing. There would be a curse. The consequence of disobedience is in Deuteronomy 30:17-20.

> *But if your heart turns away so that you do not hear, and are drawn away, and worship other gods and serve them, I announce to you today that you shall surely perish; you shall not prolong your days in the land which you cross over the Jordan to go in and possess. I call heaven and earth as witnesses today against you, that I have set before you life and death, blessing and cursing; therefore choose life, that both you and your descendants may live; that you may love Yahweh your God, that you may obey His voice, and that you may cling to Him, for He is your life and the length of your days; and that you may dwell in the land which Yahweh swore to your fathers, to Abraham, Isaac, and Jacob, to give them.*

Israel broke their covenant promise of obedience shortly after they ratified the Covenant. Moses had gone up the mountain to receive the two tablets of the testimony.[19] While he was on the mountain, the people of Israel made a golden calf and worshiped it.[20] This act broke the covenant. A basic stipulation in the covenant was, "You shall have no other gods before Me."[21] When Moses came down the mountain and was confronted with the apostasy, he broke the tablets.[22] This destruction signified the end of the covenant relationship. The actual invalidation of the covenant was the result of the apostasy.[23] Immediately the covenant breakers became subject to the curse threatened in the treaty. The only remedy was repentance and submission to the covenant granter.

Moses' prayer of repentance[24] was accepted by Yahweh and the covenant was renewed.[25] This renewal established a pattern in Israel; whenever the covenant was broken it had to be renewed. Israel knew the covenant was broken when the shalom (peace) associated with the covenant ceased and when Yahweh said that it had been broken.

Israel knew the covenant was broken when the *shalom* (peace) associated with the covenant ceased and when Yahweh said that it had been broken.

Herein lies a significant insight for us in our covenant relationship with God. Some believers often remark, "I feel at peace over this decision. That's how I know I'm doing the right thing and God is in it." Really? Our feelings can deceive us. Shalom (peace) with God exists when He says it's "peace" not when we feel self-righteous, justified, and "at peace." Peace only truly exists when those in covenant with Yahweh are obedient to His ways.

Covenant Renewal

The covenant was also renewed in connection with the transfer of authority. Such a renewal took place when Moses transferred his leadership to Joshua.[26] The covenant renewals which took place at the end of Joshua's life[27] and at the institution of the monarchy[28] show that the concern was ensuring the continuity of the covenant. The change in leadership did not diminish the covenantal obligations of the nation nor the blessings and cursings within the covenant.

The renewal of Joshua 24 contains a preamble, an antecedent history, statement of purpose, witnesses, and curses. In the statement of purpose[29] the relationship is defined negatively and positively. Israel was to put away the gods served in Egypt and serve Yahweh. Yahweh had blessed Israel by bringing them into the land.[30] If they did not fulfill their covenantal obligation then Yahweh would consume them and do them harm. This covenant arrangement was accepted by the people and solemnized by an oath.[31] Joshua wrote the covenant in a book and set up a stone as a witness.

Likewise, we are called to put away the gods of our self-centered, idolatrous culture and "serve the Lord" in our Egypt. The intrusive gods proffered to us by media, politics, the arts, education, and materialism must be silenced so we can hear the "still, small voice of God" as well as the prophets in our midst. Like Samuel, they speak of the ways and will of the Lord in our midst. The book within our midst is the New Testament or New Covenant and the stone is the chief Cornerstone—Jesus Christ.

At the end of the era of the judges, Samuel gathered all Israel at Gilgal to renew the kingdom.[32] The kingdom to be renewed is best understood as the kingdom of Yahweh. The people had approached Samuel and asked for a king "like all the nations."[33] This request broke the terms of the covenant for the people were rejecting Yahweh as their king.[34] Consequently the gathering at Gilgal was not only to renew the covenant at a time of transfer of leadership, but also to restore the covenant following covenant failure.

Samuel's recitation of antecedent history recounts Yahweh's saving acts in contrast to Israel's sin.[35] The request for a king demonstrates a disregard for the previous acts of Yahweh that demonstrated His covenant faithfulness. The people preferred to rely on a human king rather than rely on Yahweh who had promised that He would be an enemy to the enemies of Israel[36] and that He would lead them and fight for them in battle.[37] Israel's request for a king reproached Yahweh, the Covenantor.

Yahweh had instructed Samuel to give Israel a king[38] and had revealed to Samuel who should be king. The king had been set over the people by Yahweh and was responsible to obey Yahweh.[39] The king would be subject to the authority of Yahweh and bound by the same covenant that bound the people to Yahweh. Absolute loyalty to Yahweh was demanded of the king and the people. Kingship was not in conflict with covenant fidelity to Yahweh.

The transfer of leadership at Gilgal was not a complete transfer. Samuel, who had been a judge, relinquished his administrative duties to the king. Nevertheless, he had the responsibility to pray for the people and to continue to instruct them.[40] A new era of administration was coming to Israel. This new administration called for a division of responsibilities, not a complete transfer. Samuel, who was to be intercessor and instructor, retained the responsibility of maintaining the *raison d'être* of Israel: "the covenant relationship with Yahweh." In retaining this responsibility, Samuel ushered in the prophetic office. H. H. Rowley points out that "the prophet was not only the man who brought the word of God to Man. He was also the spokesman of man to God...." Retaining the responsibilities of instruction and prayer, Samuel became the first prophet under the new administration of the theocracy.[41]

The Book of Judges lies between two significant Covenant Renewals: the renewal at Shechem with Joshua and the renewal at Gilgal with Samuel. According to Paul in Acts 13, the period of the Judges was four hundred fifty years. The Covenant renewal at Shechem marked the end of Joshua's leadership. The Covenant renewal at Gilgal marked the end of Samuel's service as judge and the beginning of Saul's rule as king.

> **The Book of Judges lies between two significant Covenant Renewals: the renewal at Shechem with Joshua and the renewal at Gilgal with Samuel.**

A Breach of the Covenant

The first chapter of the Book of Judges recites the failure of the sons of Israel to conquer Canaan. This failure to conquer Canaan was a breach of the covenant. Yahweh, through Moses had instructed the Sons of Israel with regard to the inhabitants of the "Promised Land." Yahweh had told them that, "*When you have crossed the Jordan into the land of Canaan, then you shall drive out all the inhabitants of the land from before you, destroy all their engraved stones, destroy all their molded images, and demolish all their high places; you shall dispossess the inhabitants of the land and dwell in it, for I have given you the land to possess. And you shall divide the land by lot as an inheritance among your families; to the larger you shall give a larger inheritance, and to the smaller you shall give a smaller inheritance; there everyone's inheritance shall be whatever falls to him by lot. You shall inherit according to the tribes of your fathers. But if you do not drive out the inhabitants of the land from before you, then it shall be that those whom you let remain shall be irritants in your eyes and thorns in your sides, and they shall harass you in the land where you dwell. Moreover it shall be that I will do to you as I thought to do to them.*"[42]

Since the Sons of Israel had not driven out the inhabitants, nor torn down their altars, Yahweh, during another Covenant renewal at Bochim, told the Sons of Israel that the inhabitants would be as thorns and the pagan gods would be a snare. This condemnation was preceded by the assertion that Yahweh would never break the covenant He had made with the Sons of Israel.

Israel had broken the Covenant shortly after it was ratified and continued to break it as Israel failed to obey Yahweh. Continual inability to keep the Covenant is a manifestation of the problem Paul speaks of in Romans and Galatians. In Romans, Paul says that while we were in our flesh the law aroused our sin. The law defined sin and set up God's standard, and man falls short of God's standard. In Galatians 3:24, Paul calls the law a tutor. According to Paul, the law leads us to Christ, the one who fulfilled the law. We are reckoned righteous when we believe in the person and work of Jesus the Christ.

Through Jesus we have peace with God and He will never leave us nor forsake us. This lasting peace transcends any thoughts or feelings of peace we may try to construct for ourselves within the struggles, trials, and tribulations of life. In fact, we may feel tremendous inner conflict and experience complete unrest all around us. Nonetheless, peace is not a lack of conflict, battles or stress. It is the witness of the Spirit of Christ within us and to His covenant community, the Church, that He is always with us, never abandoning us or forsaking us. In the midst of the struggles the peace of God that passes all understanding continues as we walk in faith and obedience to God.

So our peace with God may be broken because of sin. As was said to the Sons of Israel, God will never break the Covenant, but we may / can lose the peace of the covenant because of sin. We must "renew" the covenant by confessing our sin. Our covenant God promises that when we confess our sin He is faithful and will forgive our sin and cleanse us from all unrighteousness (1 John 1:9). The Sons of Israel had to offer sacrifices at their covenant renewals, but we do not, for the one sacrifice of Jesus cleanses us from all sin. In the midst of all of life's storms, we hear Christ saying in every moment, "Peace be still."

Ask Yourself...

- *Am I presently enjoying the Peace of the Covenant with the Father through Jesus? If not, what sins do I need to confess so that the peace of God may reign in my heart?*

- *To continually walk in His peace, what steps do I need to be taking?* (See the list below.)

Here are some action steps you can start with today. Check all that apply.

- Confess any covenant relationships that are broken in your life. What can be done to renew them?
- What can you do about broken covenant relationships in my family, church or elsewhere without being meddlesome or taking up offenses?
- Write down the blessings that are mine as a child of God and co-heir with Jesus.
- Write down the consequences that are mine if the peace of the Covenant is broken.

Chapter 3

JUDAH—ISRAEL'S PREEMINENT TRIBE

A number of years ago my wife and I determined to move closer to our parents and began to look for a pastorate within a day's drive of our parents. Through our denominational affiliation, we became aware of a small church in a medium sized city in need of a pastor. The small church had enormous potential.

Their potential included the following assets: a church building, a building with two "storefronts" and six apartments, an endowment of nearly a million dollars, and about six hundred thousand dollars to be added to the endowment upon dissolution of a very old financial instrument. The church planned to convert the apartments into either "halfway" housing or apartments to rent. The two storefronts were to be used as a bookstore and a coffeehouse. With some of the funds available, the church proposed to run a food pantry for needy people in the neighborhood. As I surveyed the church, its assets, the neighborhood, and my interests, I became very enthusiastic about the prospect of serving as pastor of such a small congregation with such great potential.

I was called to be the pastor. After being "in the saddle" for about two months, I discovered that not all was well. As I attempted to address the items that needed to be addressed, I uncovered more problems and encountered great opposition. Within two years the church summarily dismissed me. Three years later the church closed.

The denomination which oversaw the dissolution received over two million dollars. That two million dollars was used to start three church planting hubs in Massachusetts, Minnesota, and California. Many churches were planted and some are sustained even now. Furthermore, some of the money was used to upgrade the denominational headquarters. What I thought was a promised land was merely a mirage not a divine vision. I discovered that "A man's heart plans his way, But Yahweh directs his steps."[43]

God had called Moses out of the desert and sent him to Egypt to deliver the Sons of Israel out of bondage.[44] Joshua had been set apart by God to lead the Sons of Israel into the Promised Land.[45] Moses was of the Tribe of Levi, the Tribe of the Priests.[46] Joshua was of the Tribe of Ephraim, the Tribe which envied Judah's position.[47] The position of Ephraim in Israel is the position of the firstborn. Jacob bestowed the blessing of the firstborn upon Joseph, the firstborn of the favored wife Rachel.[48] Thus Joseph possessed a double portion manifested in the tribes of Manassah and Ephraim.[49] Manassah, as Joseph's firstborn received a double portion of the firstborn's blessing but Jacob's preference for Ephraim prophetically placed Ephraim in the position of authority in Israel.[50]

Throughout the history of Israel, Ephraim had a prominence among the Tribes, such that the Northern Kingdom after the division following Solomon's reign is often called Ephraim as the Southern Kingdom is called Judah.[51] But in Judges 1:2, Yahweh, the Covenant God who had revealed Himself to Moses[52] and brought the Sons of Israel out of Egypt,[53] reveals to the Sons of Israel that Judah is to lead the Sons of Israel against the Canaanites. This designation of Judah as the preeminent tribe is affirmed in Judges 20:18 as Yahweh says that Judah should go first into battle against Benjamin. Why was Judah set apart as the tribe to lead the others?

> *Now the sons of Reuben the firstborn of Israel — he was indeed the firstborn, but because he defiled his father's bed, his birthright was given to the sons of Joseph, the son of Israel, so that the genealogy is not listed according to the birthright; yet Judah prevailed over his brothers, and from him came a ruler, although the birthright was Joseph's. (1 Chronicles 5:1-2)*

Not only does the Chronicler give us a clue to Judah's place as the leader of the tribes in Judges 1, the Psalmist also provides a clue in Psalm 78:67-72.

Moreover He rejected the tent of Joseph, And did not choose the tribe of Ephraim, But chose the tribe of Judah, Mount Zion which He loved. And He built His sanctuary like the heights, Like the earth which He has established forever. He also chose David His servant, And took him from the sheep-folds; From following the ewes that had young He brought him, To shepherd Jacob His people, And Israel His inheritance. So he shepherded them according to the integrity of his heart, And guided them by the skillfulness of his hands.

The Chronicler and the Psalmist direct our thinking to understand that Yahweh set apart Judah to be the "Firstborn" tribe from which the ruler in Israel would come. This is in accord with the blessing of Judah by Jacob in Genesis 49:8-12.

Judah, you are he whom your brothers shall praise; Your hand shall be on the neck of your enemies; Your father's children shall bow down before you. Judah is a lion's whelp; From the prey, my son, you have gone up. He bows down, he lies down as a lion; And as a lion, who shall rouse him? The scepter shall not depart from Judah, Nor a lawgiver from between his feet, Until Shiloh comes; And to Him shall be the obedience of the people. Binding his donkey to the vine, And his donkey's colt to the choice vine, He washed his garments in wine, And his clothes in the blood of grapes. His eyes are darker than wine, And his teeth whiter than milk.

Judah was the fourth son of Jacob. Leah, the mother of six sons of Jacob, bore four sons before any other sons were born. The order of birth of the sons of Jacob was: Reuben, Simeon, Levi and Judah by Leah; Dan and Naphtali by Bilhah, Rachel's maid; Gad and Asher by Zilpah, Leah's maid; Issachar and Zebulun by Leah, and Joseph and Benjamin by Rachel. Reuben, Simeon, and Levi gave up their place as "firstborn" because they violated their father Jacob's trust. Reuben had carnal relations with Bilhah his father's concubine and therefore lost the preeminence of the first-born.[54] Simeon and Levi took "the law" into their own hands to defend the honor of their sister Dinah. Their deceit and treachery made them unfit for the blessing of the firstborn.[55] Thus Judah, the fourth son of Leah, receives the preeminence due the firstborn.

Jacob intended Joseph and his sons to have the preeminence. But God overruled as He had overruled in the matter of Jacob's wife. Jacob labored for seven years to have Rachel as wife. In God's Providence, Leah was given to Jacob as wife. Jacob, if he had submitted to God's design in marriage, should have been content.[56] Instead of seeing God's hand of Providence, Jacob became angry and demanded Rachel also. In pursuing Rachel as wife, Jacob not only did not follow God's design in marriage, he married an idolater.[57] Thus Judah, although fourth of Leah's sons, became the son whose sons and daughters would have preeminence in Israel.

> **But God overruled as He had overruled in the matter of Jacob's wife.**

It should be noted that the blessing upon Judah specifically stipulates in verse 10, "The sceptre should not depart from Judah, nor the ruler's staff from between his feet until Shiloh comes, and to him shall be the obedience of the peoples." This portion of Judah's blessing has two very important elements: the scepter that represents the kingly line shall remain with Judah, and one specific person will bring to an end the kings of Judah. The last king of the Judaic line will have "peoples" that is more than the Sons of Israel submitting to his reign. This one to come is Jesus who is of the Tribe of Judah and is King of kings and Lord of lords.

Therefore Judah was to rule over the tribes of Israel. Thus, Yahweh said that Judah would fill the leadership gap.[58] Caleb, being the eldest in the tribe, would be the "defacto leader." Caleb witnessed the Exodus, spied out the land, endured the forty years of wandering, and entered the land with Joshua. He was the one among all Israel who knew Yahweh and had seen the work of Yahweh.[59] He set the example for all for Caleb had "a different spirit and followed the Lord fully."[60]

> **Caleb set the example for all for he had "a different spirit and followed the Lord fully."[61]**

Caleb's example and the designation of Judah as the preeminent tribe foreshadows the coming of Jesus, the Christ. Jesus' genealogy in Matthew 1 and Luke 3 traces back through Judah. Jesus is the fulfillment of the blessing of Jacob on Judah for Jesus is the one who was to come. Therefore, Jesus, who is the firstborn from the dead, receives the blessing of the firstborn and fulfills the firstborn blessing of Judah.

In the blessing upon Judah, Jacob says, "The scepter shall not depart from Judah, nor a lawgiver from between his feet, until Shiloh comes; and to Him shall be the obedience of the peoples." This foreshadows Psalm 2:6-8 where Yahweh says," Yet I have set My King on My holy hill of Zion. I will declare the decree: Yahweh has said to Me, 'You are My Son, today I have begotten You. Ask of Me, and I will give You the nations for Your inheritance, and the ends of the earth for Your possession.'"

The Psalmist foreshadows the words of Jesus to His disciples in Matthew 28:18-20, "All authority has been given to Me in heaven and on earth. Go therefore and make disciples of all the nations, baptizing them in the name of the Father and of the Son and of the Holy Spirit, teaching them to observe all things that I have commanded you; and lo, I am with you always, even to the end of the age. Amen."

The King we serve will never be succeeded, never be overthrown, never renege on a promise, and never be defeated for He is son of Judah, Immanuel. Therefore we may boldly herald the message of the King in all the Earth.

Ask Yourself...

- *How have I seen the Lord overrule my plans? How has His rule benefited me?*
- *What consequences have I seen as a result of being discontent with God's provision?*
- *How has God revealed His faithfulness in spite of my expectations and plans?*
- *How can I help someone else understand that our God does all things well for the benefit of His people?*

Here are some action steps you can start with today. Check them off as they are completed.

- Reread the scripture passages in this chapter.
- Tell these stories in your own words so you can use them to help others see the benefits of obedience to God's covenant.
- Think of those you know who could benefit from this information.
- Ask God to reveal when and how you can use what you have learned to help these people.

Chapter 4

YAHWEH'S COVENANTAL COMMITMENT

They met as students at Columbia Bible College. Robertson McQuilkin remembers sitting behind her in chapel, watching Muriel Webendorfer run her "lovely, artistic fingers" through her "lovely, brown hair." As they began spending time together, he discovered Muriel was "delightful, smart, and gifted, and just a great lover of people and more fun than you can imagine." He proposed on Valentine's Day in 1948 and they married in August the same year. For the next three decades, they raised six children and served God together at a variety of posts, including twelve years as missionaries in Japan. In 1968 they returned to the United States and Robertson became president of Columbia Bible College (now Columbia International University). Muriel taught at the college, spoke at women's conferences, appeared on television, and was featured on a radio program that was considered for national syndication.

The first sign that their lives were about to change appeared in 1978 during a trip to Florida to visit some friends. Muriel loved to tell stories, and punctuated them with her infectious laughter. But while they were driving, she began telling a story she had just finished a few minutes earlier.

"Honey, you just told us that," Robertson said, but she laughed and went on.

"That's funny," Robertson thought. "That has never happened before."

But the same type of problem occurred again, and with increasing frequency. Muriel began to find it difficult to plan menus for parties. She would speak at public functions and lose her train of thought. She had to give up her radio show.

In 1981, when she was hospitalized for tests on her heart, a doctor told Robertson, "You may need to think about the possibility of Alzheimer's disease."

It was hard to believe, since the disease—which causes progressive degeneration of the brain—does not usually strike someone so young, but the diagnosis was confirmed by other doctors.

As the next few years went by, Robertson watched helplessly as his fun, creative, loving partner slowly faded away. Muriel knew she was having problems, but she never understood that she had Alzheimer's.

"One thing about forgetting is that you forget that you forgot. So, she never seemed to suffer too much with it," Robertson said.

Muriel found it more and more difficult to express herself. She stopped speaking in complete sentences, relying on phrases or words. Though she continued to recognize her husband and children, she lived, in Robertson's words, "in happy oblivion to almost everything else."

There was one phrase she said often, however: "I love you."

Robertson learned much about love from Muriel and from God during those first few years of her disease. When he was away from her, she became distressed, and would often walk the half-mile to his office several times a day to look for him. Once Robertson was helping take her shoes off and discovered her feet were bloody from walking. He was amazed by her love for him, and wondered if he loved God enough to be so driven to spend time with Him.

By 1990, Robertson knew he needed to make a decision about his career. The school needed him 100 percent, and Muriel needed him 100 percent. In the end, Robertson says, the choice to step down from his position was easy for him to make. Perhaps the best explanation can be found in the letter he wrote to the Columbia Bible College constituency to explain his decision:

> *...recently it has become apparent that Muriel is contented most of the time she is with me and almost none of the time I am away from her. It is not just "discontent." She is filled with fear—even terror—that she has lost me and always goes in search of me when I leave home. So it is clear to me that she needs me now, full-time...*

*The decision was made, in a way, 42 years ago when I prom-
ised to care for Muriel "in sickness and in health...till death
do us part." So, as I told the students and faculty, as a man
of my word, integrity has something to do with it. But so
does fairness. She has cared for me fully and sacrificially all
these years; if I cared for her for the next 40 years I would
not be out of her debt.*

*Duty, however, can be grim and stoic. But there is more: I
love Muriel. She is a delight to me—her childlike depen-
dence and confidence in me, her warm love, occasional
flashes of that wit I used to relish so, her happy spirit and
tough resilience in the face of her continual distressing frus-
tration. I don't have to care for her. I get to! It is a high honor
to care for so wonderful a person.*

So, Robertson became a homemaker and a care-giver, and he's
proud of it.

"The touchstone for me," he says, "has always been, whatever God has
put in me or will ever put in me, how can that count the maximum for
what He is up to in the world? People think it must be so difficult, but
actually even on the emotional side I didn't look back with any regrets
at all. I enjoyed the new life. All I had to know was God's assignment for
me now."

When Robertson accepted his new assignment, he thought his public
ministry was ending. Instead, it transformed into something altogether
different. In a culture where people prize their individual freedoms above
all else, this simple story of a man who loved and served his wife has
touched people in a way that he never anticipated.[62]

Three Covenant Issues

The ratification of the Sinaitic Covenant by the Sons of Israel meant
that they acknowledged Yahweh as King and they agreed to obey Him.
Judges chapter one and two record how the Sons of Israel failed to drive
out the inhabitants of the land. The Sons of Israel also forsook Yahweh
and served the pagan gods. According to the covenant, the Sons of Israel

were given up to discipline: "Yahweh sold them into the hands of their enemies all around so that they could no longer stand before their enemies."[63] But the incomplete conquest is demonstrably a part of the covenantal design for Yahweh. He was testing Israel.[64] The new generation had to learn war: covenant or Yahweh war. They had not seen the great victories Yahweh had procured for Israel over the Egyptians and others. Therefore Judges presents three covenantal issues: the failure of the Sons of Israel to obey their Covenant King, the discipline of the Sons of Israel as a result of their disobedience, and the revelation of the faithfulness of their Covenant King.

> **As the great King, Yahweh was committed to provide for and defend the Sons of Israel.**

As the great King, Yahweh was committed to provide for and defend the Sons of Israel. The generation that had ratified the Sinaitic Covenant and their children had seen Yahweh's provision and defense as they left Egypt, traveled from Egypt to the Promised Land, wandered in the desert for forty years, and possessed the Promised Land. As the Sons of Israel left Egypt they plundered the Egyptians.[65] As the Sons of Israel traveled to the Promised Land and wandered in the desert for forty years, Yahweh provided Manna, clothing that did not wear out, and water for their sustenance.[66] Yahweh proved Himself as Israel's defender and protector. He defeated the Egyptians while Israel kept silent,[67] gave the Canaanites, Amorites, and Bashan into the hands of Israel.[68] Jericho, Ai, and other portions of the Promised Land were given to Israel by Yahweh. But the generation that entered the era of the Judges "Did not know Yahweh nor the work which He had done for Israel."[69] As Yahweh had done for the previous generations, so He would do for the Sons of Israel during the Era of the Judges. Yahweh appears by name over one hundred and fifty times in the Book of Judges as testament to His faithfulness to the Covenant ratified at Sinai.

> **Yahweh's commitment to the covenants of the Old Testament culminates in the person of Jesus Christ.**

Yahweh's commitment to the covenants of the Old Testament culminates in the person of Jesus Christ. Paul tells us that when the fullness of the time had come, God sent forth His Son, born of a woman, born under the law. The Sinaitic Covenant ratified by the Sons of Israel is "the law" of Galatians 4:4. In this passage, Paul tells us when He was born, from whence He came, the manner in which He came, and the purpose of His coming.

According to Paul, the law was / is a schoolmaster that leads us to Christ. Within the context of Galatians, the fullness of time has to do with the appointed time for the end of the Law. Using the analogy of the home, Paul speaks of the child as being under the care of guardians and stewards. Paul speaks of those under the Law as being in bondage. The time of the Law having come to an end, God sent His Son.

The sending of the Son is in fulfillment of the Word of God throughout the Old Testament. This act of God is alluded to in the Garden of Eden when God said to the serpent, "And I will put enmity between you and the woman, and between your seed and her seed; He shall bruise your head, and you shall bruise His heel."[70] The expectation of the "Coming One" is in the Abrahamic Covenant, Davidic Covenant, the Sinaitic Covenant, and throughout the history of Israel as the nation fails in its vocation like the other nations. The intervention of God in the affairs of men throughout the Old Testament foreshadows the ultimate intervention of "the word made flesh." That is God made in the likeness of men so that God dwells with men.

Jesus (Yahweh saves), the name given to the child who is Imannuel, God with us, was born of a woman. Thus, the one who is Immanuel is truly man. As the Creed of Chalcedon states:

> *We, then, following the holy Fathers, all with one consent, teach men to confess one and the same Son, our Lord Jesus Christ, the same perfect in Godhead and also perfect in manhood; truly God and truly man, of a reasonable [rational] soul and body; consubstantial [co-essential] with the Father according to the Godhead, and consubstantial with us according to the Manhood; in all things like unto us, without sin; begotten before all ages of the Father according to the Godhead, and in these latter days, for us and for our salvation, born of the Virgin Mary, the Mother of God, according to the Manhood; one and the same Christ, Son, Lord, Only begotten, to be acknowledged in two natures, inconfusedly, unchangeably, indivisibly, inseparably; the distinction of natures being by no means*

taken away by the unity, but rather the property of each nature being preserved, and concurring in one Person and one Subsistence, not parted or divided into two persons, but one and the same Son, and only begotten, God the Word, the Lord Jesus Christ; as the prophets from the beginning [have declared] concerning him, and the Lord Jesus Christ himself has taught us, and the Creed of the holy Fathers has handed down to us.

It ought to be particularly noted that Mary (the woman in Paul's clause "born of a woman"), is the mother of Jesus' humanity not of His divinity. For Jesus was and is the eternal begotten of the Father. Furthermore, Mary acknowledged her need of a savior in Luke 1:47 when she refers to "God my Savior".

Jesus, the one who is God and who is also man, was born under the Law. The Law that was to end must be fulfilled. Jesus said, "Do not think that I came to destroy the Law or the Prophets. I did not come to destroy but to fulfill. For assuredly, I say to you, till heaven and earth pass away, one jot or one tittle will by no means pass from the law till all is fulfilled. Whoever therefore breaks one of the least of these commandments, and teaches men so, shall be called least in the kingdom of heaven; but whoever does and teaches them, he shall be called great in the kingdom of heaven. For I say to you, that unless your righteousness exceeds the righteousness of the scribes and Pharisees, you will by no means enter the kingdom of heaven."[71] As a consequence of being born under the law, Jesus learned obedience even to His death upon the cross.

Jesus was sent by the Father, born of a woman and born under the Law that God's people would be redeemed and receive the adoption of sons. As Jesus said in Matthew 5, we cannot enter the Kingdom of God unless our righteousness exceeds the righteousness of the scribes and Pharisees. It is not possible for any of us to fulfill the requirement of the Law. But, Jesus fulfilled the Law and took the penalty of the Law for those redeemed from the Law. His fulfillment of the Law is called His active obedience. His death upon the cross is called His passive obedience. When He was nailed to the cross He became a curse for us that He might bear our sin. Having fulfilled the Law, borne the penalty of the Law, He now lives seated at the right hand of the Father interceding for us; therefore we may receive the adoption of Sons. As sons of God we are co–inheritors with Jesus. What do we inherit? We inherit eternal life and all the blessings of the new heaven and new earth. Jesus is our elder brother, being the firstborn from the dead. The writer to the Hebrews summarizes all this.

Therefore, when He came into the world, He said:

> *"Sacrifice and offering You did not desire,*
> *But a body You have prepared for Me.*
> *In burnt offerings and sacrifices for sin*
> *You had no pleasure.*
> *Then I said, 'Behold, I have come —*
> *In the volume of the book it is written of Me —*
> *To do Your will, O God.'"*

> *Previously saying, "Sacrifice and offering, burnt offerings, and offerings for sin You did not desire, nor had pleasure in them" (which are offered according to the law), then He said, "Behold, I have come to do Your will, O God." He takes away the first that He may establish the second. By that will we have been sanctified through the offering of the body of Jesus Christ once for all.*

> *And every priest stands ministering daily and offering repeatedly the same sacrifices, which can never take away sins. But this Man, after He had offered one sacrifice for sins forever, sat down at the right hand of God, from that time waiting till His enemies are made His footstool. For by one offering He has perfected forever those who are being sanctified. (Hebrews 10:5-14)*

Let us remember that the good news of the birth and life of Jesus is rooted in the reason He came. He came to fulfill all righteousness that we may have life.

Dear Reader, as we continue to meditate on the Book of Judges, remember that the law was given through Moses; grace and truth were realized through Jesus Christ. As Yahweh's faithfulness is revealed throughout Judges, so too His faithfulness is revealed in the New Testament and in your daily life. The promise that He would always keep the Covenant with Israel is the same promise He gives you. As He gave Himself as a shield and great reward to Abraham and defended and provided for the Sons of Israel, so He has promised that He will never forsake us and that no created thing can separate us from His

Let us remember that the good news of the birth and life of Jesus is rooted in the reason He came. He came to fulfill all righteousness that we may have life.

love. You may be under discipline, but that is cause for rejoicing, for the Lord disciplines His children. Rejoice under discipline, for discipline is proof that you are loved. It is also necessary to conform you into the image of the firstborn, even Jesus the Christ.

Ask Yourself...

- *What commitments have I made? Do I keep my commitments?*
- *How has God's commitment to me through Jesus been demonstrated in my life?*
- *Am I able to tell (bear witness) of God's faithfulness?*
- *How do I see God's loving care manifested in my church, my family, and my life?*
- *What in my life is cause for God to be patient with me?*
- *What have I not learned?*
- *How do I point others to the God who has committed to men His tender care, love, and compassion?*

Here are some action steps you can start with today.

- List those who are currently in the midst of trials in their lives.
- Ask God to show you how to reveal His tender care, love, and compassion for them.
- Watch for divine appointments with these people and follow the prompting of the Holy Spirit to minister to them.
- Begin keeping a journal of the amazing ways God uses you to minister to others from what you have learned about God.

Chapter 5

DIVINE PROVISION FOR LEADERSHIP

Once upon a time a young man, as he was laboring in his father's field, was contemplating his future. Having been taught that he ought to "seek the Lord's will," he prayed and asked for a sign. As he continued to work in his father's field in the next few weeks, he continued to ask the Lord for a sign. A number of weeks went by with no apparent answer to his prayer. He talked about his prayer with his parents and they encouraged him to continue to pray and wait upon the Lord.

He continued to pray and wait. One day, laying on his back during his lunch break, he noticed a distinct formation in the clouds. He looked earnestly and was convinced that the Lord was giving him an answer to his prayer. The formation he saw were two very large letters P C. Ah, he thought, I am to preach Christ.

At the end of the day he went home, told his parents and prepared to go off to study for the ministry. He spent the next few weeks investigating schools. He spoke to his pastor who thought his enthusiasm was refreshing. The pastor suggested a school and wrote a glowing letter of introduction for him. He was accepted.

He went off to the school with great hope of fulfilling his calling. He found the work arduous and very frustrating. There was no joy for him. One of his professors noted that he was having great difficulty and was becoming very depressed. The professor asked him to stop by his office for a chat. The young man agreed.

Upon arrival, the young man sat down with some apprehension. The professor, a genial man who had been discipling young men for over forty years, asked the young man why he came to the school. A reiteration of the weeks of prayer, waiting, the sign in the heavens, and the pastor's encouragement unfolded.

Having listened intently, the professor asked, "Did you enjoy working on your father's farm?"

The young man grinned from ear to ear and said, "O my, yes!"

The professor then inquired about life on the farm and what in particular brought the young man joy. Out gushed a torrent of tasks the young man found challenging and joyful: helping a cow birth a calf, feeding the chickens, watching seeds germinate and grow until the fruit was ready to harvest, the rest in the evening after a hard day of labor, eating a hearty meal that was representative of the labor on the farm, and the joy of selling to others the produce of the farm. The professor then inquired about those aspects of farm life that brought pain and sorrow. The young man thought for a moment and said that the joys were far more than the sorrows.

Having heard the young man's story and answers to his questions, the professor said, "What joys do you have here?"

The young man was very still as he contemplated the question. Finally, he said, "None."

The professor then asked, "What sorrows come upon you here?"

The young man looked at the floor as tears welled up in his eyes. Very softly, nearly inaudibly, the young man said that he had nothing but misery.

Having heard the young man's confession of pain, the professor got up from his chair, walked over to the young man, put his arm around him, and said, "Son, I believe that you misunderstood God's answer to your prayer. The sign in the heavens did not mean 'Preach Christ.' The sign was telling you to 'Plant corn.'"

As a result of breaching the Covenant, the Sons of Israel were given over to oppression and affliction, but this discipline was not terminal, for Yahweh raised up Judges. The Judges were raised up to deliver and to rule. They were to lead Israel in the same manner as Moses and Joshua. These that Yahweh raised up to deliver were to have a prophetic function, for we are told that the Sons of Israel did not listen to the judges.[72] The judges exercising a prophetic function would also be consistent with Yahweh's claim that He daily sent His servants the prophets from the Exodus to the Exile.[73] To understand how the Judges were involved in prophetic activity, it will be helpful to understand why prophets existed and the role of the prophet within the nation of Israel.

Following the giving of "The Decalogue," the people approached Moses with the request that Moses, not God, should speak with the people. Yahweh had spoken directly to the people. The confrontation with Yahweh had caused the people to tremble and fear for their lives.[74] The intent of the assembling had been to instill in the people an awe (fear) of Yahweh so that they would not sin. Each member of the covenant people was at that moment in the position of receiving Yahweh's revelation, but the direct address was more than the nation wished to bear. Therefore, they asked Moses to continue as the one who brought Yahweh's word to the people. The people wanted Moses as a mediator. This mediatory role meant that the prophet was to speak for Yahweh to the people and to speak to Yahweh on behalf of the people.

The words of the prophets spoken to the people were understood to be the words of Yahweh.

The relationship that existed between Moses, Yahweh, and the people is best illustrated by the relationship between Aaron, Moses, and Pharaoh.[75] Aaron was the one who spoke to Pharaoh. Words spoken by Aaron to Pharaoh were understood to be the words of Moses. In like manner, the words of the prophets spoken to the people were understood to be the words of Yahweh.

Israel eventually lost the ability to "inquire of the Lord."[76] Before this tragic end came upon Israel, the prophets brought the word of Yahweh in various ways. The prophets were from varied backgrounds, involved themselves in society at different levels, and addressed various people and issues in society.

God in His wisdom established guidelines for the covenant people for determining who was or could be a true spokesman for Yahweh. These include a call to an Israelite who was to speak the words of Yahweh, not one word being false.[77] Jeremiah states that the appointment by Yahweh is decisive in determining who is false or true[78] (this appointment is understood as the "prophetic call"). The supposition is if they had stood in Yahweh's counsel then they would have spoken Yahweh's words, turning the people from sin.

If, as Jeremiah implies, the call of the prophet is decisive, it is curious that the scripture contains the call of only seven prophets. The seven who have their calls recorded are Moses, Samuel, Elisha, Isaiah, Jeremiah, Ezekiel, and Amos. In each case the message carried was of "earth-shaking" proportions to the established order. A brief look at each of these calls may demonstrate that some justification was necessary.

Moses' commission was to go into Egypt and bring Israel out of Egypt into the land of Canaan and to worship Yahweh at Sinai.[79] This act of God was to be the cornerstone of a covenantal relationship with Israel. Moses, knowing that he would have to speak with authority, asked for some identification from God. At this point God reveals His covenant name, Yahweh.

Samuel received his call as a young boy in the service of the Temple. No theophany, such as the burning bush, accompanied this call. The voice of God called to Samuel four times. Samuel was not able to discern that it was the voice of God. The priest made that discernment for him after the third time.[80] There are two elements that may justify the recording of Samuel's call. The first would be the rarity of the word of Yahweh at the time. The second would be Samuel's age and the apparent circumvention of Yahweh's present representative, Eli, the priest.

> **The call of the prophet is decisive for a true prophet of Yahweh would speak Yahweh's words, turning the people from sin.**

Elisha's call followed the dramatic contest on Mount Carmel. Following the contest and refreshment in the desert, Elijah was charged with the responsibility to anoint a prophet who would take his place. Elisha, his replacement, ministered to Elijah and received a double portion of Elijah's spirit. According to the word given to Elijah, the ministry of Elisha was to coincide with the rule of Hazael in Syria and Jehu in Israel. Their activity was to result in a purge of Israel. Elisha's ministry included help and solace to non-Israelites as well as the oppressed in Israel. Elisha spoke words of Judgment and ministered to a "remnant" in Israel.[81]

The three calls reviewed above do not include visions in the account. God called Moses using a theophany. He spoke to Samuel using a priest to discern the call. Another prophet was used to call Elisha. The calls of Isaiah, Jeremiah, and Ezekiel all include a vision. Each accompanying vision is germane to the message that was entrusted to the prophet. Isaiah's vision was of the Lord sitting upon His throne and seraphim calling out, "Holy, Holy, Holy, is Yahweh of hosts, the whole earth is full of His glory."[82] Isaiah's commission was to result in a national insensitivity to Yahweh, and the subsequent devastation of the land. Ultimately a holy stump would be preserved.

The almond tree and boiling pot visions accompanying the call of Jeremiah reinforce the charge to "pluck up and to break down, to destroy and to overthrow, to build and to plant."[83] As Jeremiah's ministry developed, it embroiled him in false charges, prison, and life threatening situations. He was indeed "a fortified city and an iron pillar, and bronze walls against the whole land."[84] Jeremiah's ministry was to prepare Jerusalem and Judea for exile. This was a message the people did not want to hear.

Most detailed and mystifying of the three visions is Ezekiel's vision. A vision of four figures and the glory of God are a prelude to a commission which puts Ezekiel in a position of speaking the words of Yahweh without regard for the effect on the hearers.[85] Later Ezekiel sees the glory of God depart the Temple and Jerusalem just prior to their destruction.[86]

Each of these calls represents a direction in the activity of Yahweh that would be different than expected by those who were conscious of the relationship of Yahweh and the covenant people. Through Isaiah, Yahweh rejects the nation and establishes a remnant (holy stump). Jeremiah tells the people that capitulation to the enemy is the only way to preserve themselves. As a result Jeremiah is branded a traitor and imprisoned.[87] The destruction of the Temple and the city of Jerusalem, and the word that those in exile were the Lord's preservation set Ezekiel apart.[88] Each of these prophets represents another step in God's putting aside the nation of Israel in favor of a "remnant" as a result of the rebellion and disobedience of the covenant people. Justification to the audience or encouragement for the prophet or the faithful few may have necessitated the writing down of these calls.

Amos' call is referred to in Amos 7:14-15. Amaziah had sent word to King Jeroboam that Amos was conspiring against the king. Amaziah then tells Amos to return to Judah. Amos' response is a pithy account of his call. He had been a rancher and a farmer, but Yahweh removed him from those tasks. The charge given to Amos was, "Go prophesy to my people Israel." If Amos returned to Judah at the word of Amaziah, he would be disobedient to the commission entrusted to him by Yahweh.

Each call has the following elements:
- *Divine Confrontation*
- *Introductory Word*

- *Commission*
- *Objection*
- *Reassurance*
- *Sign of Confirmation*

The confrontation and the ensuing dialogue may be a result of the burden that the prophet would bear. Being a prophet meant that the individual would be under the constraint of God. A few glimpses are given of the tension and agony a prophet endured. Jeremiah complains that he was deceived.[89] Amos asks the rhetorical question, "The lion has roared–who is not afraid. The Lord Yahweh has spoken–who does not prophesy?"[90] Since Jeremiah considered the call of Yahweh decisive, it is assumed that all true prophets experienced a call.

Another concern expressed by Jeremiah was the content of the message given by the false prophets. Part of the message Jeremiah had to give contained the declaration that the "prophets prophesy falsely."[91] Apparently there were those who were saying, "You will not see the sword nor will you have famine, but I will give you lasting peace in this place."[92] Such a message would be consonant with the

A hallmark of the true prophet was the veracity of the words spoken by him.

popular understanding of the covenantal relationship between Yahweh and Israel. The land had been promised to Israel as an inheritance. The people remembered Yahweh's promises, but not their obligations within the framework of those promises. Such a message was not the truth. Those who gave the message must be false prophets. Yahweh's word was always true.

A hallmark of the true prophet was the veracity of the word spoken by him.[93] This test is dramatically demonstrated in the confrontation between Jeremiah and Hananiah. There was no obvious way that an impartial observer could determine who was speaking the truth and who was not while they debated. But the exchange ends with Jeremiah saying that Hananiah would die within the year. The record closes with the statement that Hananiah died that year in the seventh month. Consequently, Jeremiah is authenticated as the true prophet of Yahweh.[94]

False prophets were also involved in leading the people of Yahweh after strange gods. It was possible for a false prophet to perform a wonder or speak a true word. Such activity did not authenticate him as a true prophet if he led the people away from Yahweh.[95] Counseling rebellion and leading the people away from the commandments of Yahweh were marks distinguishing a false prophet.

From the available evidence and the inference in Deuteronomy 18:15, 18 it is possible to conclude that all true prophets were to be members of the covenant people, Israel. Balaam is the only noteworthy non-Israelite prophet. The scripture's own critique of him is that, "Yahweh your God was not willing to listen to Balaam,"[96] and that Balaam's way was the way of error.[97] This criterion was apparently recognized by the Israelites because the false prophets were also, apparently, Israelites.

Normalcy in Israel was to be determined by the Law given at Mount Sinai. The prophets addressed aberrations. These words were given as a result of failure to comply with Yahweh's revelation or as a preventative measure ensuring compliance with the will of God.[98] More detailed messages, similar in nature, are contained in the "Latter Prophets." Each prophet spoke to a particular time yet within an ongoing tradition / cult. The cult or "ancient inherited tradition" is comprised of the obligations enumerated in the Sinaitic Covenant.

But more than the sacrifices and other laws governing ritual and symbol, Yahweh's interest is the God-Man and Man-Man relationships. The words which Yahweh spoke directly to the people, "The Decalogue," pertain to both relationships. Jesus of Nazareth summed up the Law by quoting from the Law: "You shall love the Lord your God with all your heart, and with all your soul, and with all your mind."[99] "You shall love your neighbor as yourself."[100]

Yahweh's concern is obedience not sacrifice, as the prophets had occasion to point out.[101] The concern of the prophets, in word or deed, was the covenant Yahweh had with the people of Israel. Each of the prophets spoke within the content of the covenant relationship that was supposed to exist. Each judgment was the result of failure to comply with the terms of the covenant. Words that spoke of restoration and renewal were couched in covenantal terms. Jeremiah even spoke of a new covenant to be inscribed upon the hearts of the people.[102] Ezekiel presents the idea that individuals will be held accountable to Yahweh, as opposed to a national accountability.[103] The focus of all prophetic activity was calling the people back to their covenantal responsibilities.[104]

The prophets were primarily concerned with the covenantal obligations of the Sons of Israel. Each word of judgment, warning or encouragement was in the context of covenantal breach or obedience. Instructions (Obed in 2 Chronicles 28:9) may have been given to address a particular issue, but all was done within the framework of the covenantal responsibilities that Israel had freely accepted at Sinai. If the judges fulfilled a prophetic role in Israel, then the criteria to be a judge should be the same as the criteria to be a prophet, and the judges should be active in confronting covenantal abrogation and teaching covenantal obligation.

As representatives of Yahweh, the judges were raised up by Yahweh.[105] This text does not explain how Yahweh raised them up, but some scriptural material does. The text does contain the "call" of three judges: Gideon, Samson, and Samuel. Two others, Ehud and Othniel, are said to have been raised up by Yahweh although the author does not provide the details. Shamgar and Tola are said to have delivered Israel placing them in the sphere of Yahweh's activity since He raised up judges for the purpose of delivering the Sons of Israel from oppression.[106] The calls of Deborah, a prophetess, and the other judges are assumed. If the raising up or "call" of the judge by Yahweh was the determinant for placing the person in the position of judge, why are only three "calls" recorded? Possible justification for including the three-recorded calls will be proffered after an examination of each call.

Gideon's Call (Judges 6:11-24)

1. *Divine Confrontation*
   The Angel of Yahweh, the one who had gone from Gilgal to Bochim,[107] confronted Gideon as he threshed his wheat in hiding. This person was not a created being as is evident from the author's use of the name Yahweh in Judges 6:14-16 and His own pronouncement, "I will be with thee."

2. *Introductory Word*
   "Yahweh is with you, O valiant warrior," are the words of greeting given to Gideon. A similar salutation was used by Boaz.[108] Gideon's response challenges the salutation. With his reply, Gideon manifests that he is one who had not seen the work which Yahweh had done for Israel.

49

3. *Commission*

Gideon is commissioned to go and deliver Israel. He was to go in strength for Yahweh was sending him. Gideon had been commanded to deliver Israel from the oppression of the Midianites by Yahweh.

4. *Objection*

Gideon claims that he is from an insignificant portion of Manasseh and that he has no weapon. His claim to be from a low status in society is more superficial than real. He is able to call upon ten servants[109] and his brothers had the look of princes.[110]

5. *Reassurance*

In response to Gideon's reluctance Yahweh promised that He would be with Gideon. This same promise was given to Moses at the burning bush[111] and to Joshua when he assumed the leadership in Israel.[112] Gideon, with Yahweh as his companion, would smite the Midianites as though they were one man. This reassurance reduced the enemy to a manageable size for the one who was to deliver Israel.

6. *Sign*

Gideon, perceiving who the messenger was, asked for a sign. He prepared a sacrifice: meat, unleavened bread,[113] and broth. These were consumed by fire that sprang from the rock. The fire was a token of acceptance and a demonstration of Yahweh's power. Gideon later received confirmation through the sign of the fleece[114] and the interpretation of a dream.[115]

Samson's Call (Judges 13:3-23)

This call narrative is unique among the call narratives of the prophets and the judges. Samson's call was given to his parents prior to his birth. This is analogous to the call narratives of John the Baptist[116] and Jesus.[117]

1. *Divine Confrontation*

Here as in Judges 6, the Angel of Yahweh appears to the recipient of the call. In this case it is not the one called to be a judge, but his mother.

2. *Introductory Word*

The Angel acknowledges the woman's barrenness and tells her that she will no longer be barren. Similar announcements were made to Sarah,[118] Hannah,[119] and Zacharias, husband of Elizabeth.[120] In each instance Yahweh intervened in the life of a barren woman, and she had the privilege of being the mother of one of Yahweh's choice servants.

3. *Commission*

The child who was to be born was to be a Nazarite from birth. Usually the Nazarite vow was taken voluntarily for a specified period of time.[121] This child was to be a Nazarite "from the womb." Consequently the mother was to adhere to the stipulations of the vow during the time of gestation. The child was commissioned to "begin to deliver Israel from the Philistines."

4. *Objection*

Manoah or his wife made no objections. Manoah does ask for instructions.

5. *Reassurance*

The Angel of Yahweh appeared a second time. He spoke to Manoah placing special emphasis on the woman's responsibility during the time of gestation.

6. *Sign*

Manoah hospitably offered to make a meal for the Angel although he did not know that the angel was the Angel of Yahweh. The messenger distanced Himself from Manoah and suggested strongly that an offering be made to Yahweh. The offering was made. While the offering was being consumed the Angel ascended. During the process of offering the sacrifice, the Angel revealed His person. The revelation was veiled, but sufficient to make Manoah and his wife loyal vassals.

Samuel's Call (1 Samuel 3:4-4:1a)

1. *Divine Confrontation*

At a time when a word from Yahweh was rare and visions were scarce, Yahweh called Samuel. Samuel, in the service of Yahweh at the sanctuary, did not recognize the voice of the one who called.

51

Eli, Yahweh's representative at the time (he was priest and judge)[122] and had the discernment to know that Yahweh was calling Samuel. The double vocative, Samuel, Samuel, places Samuel in the company of Abraham,[123] Jacob,[124] and Moses.[125] All of these addresses marked important events in the lives of these significant men in Israel's history.

2. *Introductory Word*
   The word which Samuel received was a judgment on Eli and his house. Eli's sons had behaved wickedly and Eli had not rebuked them. This was the first word Samuel received as a prophet of Yahweh.

3. *Commission*
   No specific commission was given to Samuel, but his report to Eli placed him in the position of fulfilling the commission of a prophet: bearing the word of Yahweh to the people of Israel.

4. *Objection*
   There was none.

5. *Reassurance*
   The only reassurance given to Samuel was the confirmation by Eli that Yahweh had spoken.

6. *Sign*
   The only sign available was the confirmation of Samuel as a prophet of Yahweh: "Yahweh ... let none of his words fall to the ground."

Why were these calls recorded? No definitive answers can be given, but the following are possible explanations.

The Gideon narrative marks a significant change in the judge narratives. He is the last judge credited with providing rest to the land[126] and the first judge to engage in strife against Israel.[127] Gideon is the only judge whose conflict with idolatry is recorded,[128] but after his victory over Midian he made an ephod after which "all Israel played the harlot" and "... it became a snare to Gideon and his household."[129] The Gideon narrative is not only interested in the decline of the people, but also with the religious and political decline in the judges. Gideon not only delivered Israel from Midian, he also led them into civil strife and idolatry. This major change in a judge's behavior presents cause for the recording of his call.

Samson is unique among the judges. He does not lead the Sons of Israel into battle, but engages in personal vendettas. His mission was not to deliver Israel from the oppressor, but to begin to deliver Israel. His immoral behavior belied his Nazarite vow, which consecrated him to the service of Yahweh. Samson's uniqueness and disregard for the elements of his vow are items that may have necessitated the recording of his call.

Samuel is the only judge who is known to be active during the lifetime of another judge.[130] His activity during the lifetime of Eli was probably limited to bringing the word of Yahweh to Israel. After Eli died Samuel assumed the administrative duties that he later relinquished to Saul.[131] He was a pivotal person in the history of Israel: the last judge,[132] the first prophet of the new era,[133] and the one who anointed the first two kings in the new theocratic order.[134] His position at the end of one theocratic order and at the beginning of another warranted the recording of his call.

> **All the prophets and Judges foreshadow the One that God sent into the world to save the world, Jesus.**

All the prophets and judges foreshadow the One that God sent into the world to save the world. Jesus said, "I have many things to say and to judge concerning you, but He who sent Me is true; and I speak to the world those things which I heard from Him.... I do nothing of Myself; but as My Father taught Me, I speak these things. And He who sent Me is with Me. The Father has not left Me alone, for I always do those things that please Him."[135] As all other prophets, Jesus was sent to speak the words of God to men. In speaking God's word to men, Jesus confronted men in their sin and spoke to them about their obligations to God and man (Matthew 5-7 succinctly addresses all).

Jesus' Call (Luke 1)

The elements of the call are as follows:

1. *Divine Confrontation*
   Gabriel saying, "Rejoice, highly favored one, the Lord is with you; blessed are you among women!"
2. *Introductory Word*
   "Do not be afraid, Mary, for you have found favor with God."

3. *Commission*
   "And behold, you will conceive in your womb and bring forth a Son, and shall call His name Jesus. He will be great, and will be called the Son of the Highest; and the Lord God will give Him the throne of His father David. And He will reign over the house of Jacob forever, and of His kingdom there will be no end."

4. *Objection*
   "How can this be, since I do not know a man?"

5. *Reassurance*
   "The Holy Spirit will come upon you, and the power of the Highest will overshadow you; therefore, also, that Holy One who is to be born will be called the Son of God."

6. *Sign of Confirmation*
   "Now indeed, Elizabeth your relative has also conceived a son in her old age; and this is now the sixth month for her who was called barren. "For with God nothing will be impossible."
   Humble acceptance of call. "Behold the maidservant of the Lord! Let it be to me according to your word." And the angel departed from her.

Dear Reader, having considered the role of the prophet and the criteria for speaking for God, have you ever thought of yourself as a prophet of God? As you contemplate, consider the words of Moses, "Are you zealous for my sake? Oh, that all Yahweh's people were prophets and that Yahweh would put His Spirit upon them!"[136] For all of Yahweh's people to speak for Yahweh would necessitate each person: being called, knowing Yahweh's counsel, confronting covenant breach, and directing men to fulfill covenantal obligations. If Moses expressed the desire for such intimacy by all of Yahweh's people, is it not conceivable that the reality of the New Covenant in Christ Jesus provides for a prophetic role for each of God's children?

As a member of the body of Christ you have been called.[137] Your calling goes beyond your work to your total lifestyle as a witness to Jesus Christ being light and salt in the world. As a member of the body of Christ you are to: reprove, rebuke, instruct, exhort, and proclaim so that others may be equipped and respond to the Word of God. As you study the Bible you are growing in the grace and knowledge of Jesus and therefore you know the truth and ought to be discerning and teach others the same. If you "speak the truth in love" and "speak that others receive grace," you are doing the work of a prophet.

Ask Yourself...

- *Having been "called out of darkness" into the "marvelous light" of God, am I living each day in that light?*
- *Having been called by God to be His child, am I resting in Him, having cast all my cares upon Him?*
- *How does my being called out of darkness influence my thinking and behavior? Do other people know that I am walking in the "Light"?*
- *Do I speak God's words into other people's lives?*

Here are some action steps you can start with today.

- Reprove, rebuke, instruct, exhort, and proclaim God's Word so that others may be equipped and respond to the Word of God.
- Study the Bible so you will grow in the grace and knowledge of Jesus.
- Teach others what you have learned.
- Speak the truth in love so that others receive God's grace.

Chapter 6

Presence and Power of Yahweh

Home on furlough, a missionary gathered with a few of his supporters to speak of his work on the field. During the course of his presentation, he told of a trip he had taken with a fellow missionary. They had to travel to a village that was more than a day's walk so they had to spend the night in the jungle. Knowing that this was not a wise thing to do, but having no alternative they committed their night to the Lord.

Arriving at their destination the following day, a stranger came up to them and asked where the other nine fellows were. Taken aback, the missionary told the stranger that it was just two of them who traveled through the jungle. The stranger then told how he and his comrades had come upon the two sleeping missionaries, but could not approach them because there were nine men guarding them.

One of the men in the audience interrupted and asked what day and time this occurred. The missionary told him the day. The questioner then said that he was praying for the missionary at that time. Then one by one eight more men stood and told how they had been praying at that time also.

In Numbers 11:29 Moses said, "Are you zealous for my sake? Oh, that all Yahweh's people were prophets and that Yahweh would put His Spirit upon them!" In expressing the desire that all of Yahweh's people be prophets, he acknowledged that Yahweh's Spirit was necessary for men to be Yahweh's spokesmen. So too, the judges were to be

> "Are you zealous for my sake? Oh, that all Yahweh's people were prophets and that Yahweh would put His Spirit upon them!"

empowered by Yahweh's spirit. In the summary given in Judges 2:11-19, the author stipulates, "Yahweh was with the judge." The work of deliverance necessitated supernatural power. The same person who empowered Moses[138] and Joshua[139] empowered the judges. The work of deliverance given to Moses[140] and the judges[141] was the work of Yahweh.[142] The most important act of deliverance in the life of Israel was the deliverance from slavery in Egypt. All other acts of deliverance were analogous to the great deliverance from Egypt. Therefore to accomplish the work of Yahweh, the judges were empowered by the one who called them to the task. The author specifically states that the spirit came upon Othniel,[143] clothed Gideon,[144] was on Jephthah,[145] and came mightily upon Samson.[146]

Not all the judges are said to have been empowered by Yahweh's spirit. Othniel, the first judge, sets the pattern for all the other judges. An important part of the pattern is the presence of Yahweh with the judge enabling the judge to fulfill his responsibilities. Since the first judge was given Yahweh's spirit, it is to be assumed that all the judges possessed a portion of Yahweh's spirit. The pattern is reinforced at crucial junctures in the narratives. The author states that Gideon was "clothed" with the spirit of Yahweh after Gideon had destroyed the altar of Baal, and just prior to the gathering of Israelites to do battle with the Midianites. Jephthah is also said to possess the spirit of Yahweh just prior to battle. Three times the author states that Yahweh's spirit "came mightily" on Samson. Each time it precedes a feat of strength. Samson is the only judge of whom it is said that Yahweh had left him.[147] .

What a great tragedy! Yahweh left Samson.

What a great tragedy! Yahweh left Samson. When the Spirit of Yahweh came upon an individual, that individual was able to do something that was far beyond the person's physical capabilities or expectation. Consider the greatest marathoner of all: Elijah out running Ahab's chariots in I Kings 18:46. But when Yahweh left Samson the strength of Yahweh that coursed through Samson was gone, and Samson was left to do all in his own strength. Let us pause and reflect.

Jesus, the only begotten of God, became man. As man, Jesus was empowered and led by the Spirit of God. "... Jesus was led up by the Spirit into the wilderness to be tempted by the devil."[148] Jesus, following His baptism, was full of the Spirit who led (impelled or drove) Jesus to go to the wilderness to be tempted. The temptation in the wilderness was the Devil's attempt to entice Jesus to achieve the Messianic goal without enduring the cross. Throughout Jesus' ministry Satan attacked Jesus for Jesus had entered the strong man's house and had to bind the strong man so that the house could be plundered. Jesus ultimately destroyed Satan, the strong man, through His death upon the cross.[149] Yet it was the Spirit of God who filled Jesus and led Him into the wilderness. Following His temptation, Jesus returned to Galilee empowered by the Spirit.[150]

Having returned to Galilee, Jesus went to His hometown of Nazareth and entered the Synagogue on the Sabbath and read from Isaiah. Jesus read, "The Spirit of the Lord Yahweh is upon Me, because He has anointed Me to preach the gospel to the poor; He has sent Me to heal the broken-hearted, to proclaim liberty to the captives, and recovery of sight to the blind, to set at liberty those who are oppressed; to proclaim the acceptable year of Yahweh."[151] Having read the prophetic word, Jesus asserts, "Today this Scripture is fulfilled in your hearing."

When the Pharisees took counsel together to destroy Jesus, He spoke to those who followed Him quoting from Isaiah 42:1-4, "Behold! My Servant whom I have chosen, My Beloved in whom My soul is well pleased! I will put My Spirit upon Him, and He will declare justice to the Gentiles. He will not quarrel nor cry out, nor will anyone hear His voice in the streets. A bruised reed He will not break, and smoking flax He will not quench, till He sends forth justice to victory; and in His name Gentiles will trust."[152] At the beginning of His ministry and while under attack, Jesus claims to be anointed by the Spirit of Yahweh. John the Baptist, as he bears witness to the person and origin of Jesus, states that Jesus has the Spirit "without measure."[153]

The early church also acknowledged that Jesus was empowered by the Spirit of God. In his second volume to Theophilus, Luke says, "The former account I made, O Theophilus, of all that Jesus began both to do and teach, until the day in which He was taken up, after He through the Holy Spirit had given commandments to the apostles whom He had chosen, to whom He also presented Himself alive after His suffering by many infallible proofs, being seen by them during forty days and speaking of the things pertaining to the kingdom of God."[154] Luke, who had made careful inquiry, referred to his previous work, the Gospel of Luke, as containing what Jesus began both to do and to teach. The implication is that the second volume, Acts, is a record of what the ascended Jesus continues to do and teach. Luke states that Jesus, through the Holy Spirit, gave commandments to the apostles. Once again, the implication is that the continuing work of the ascended Jesus will be accomplished through the same Spirit.

As he gives an account of the early Church, Luke records Peter's presentation of the Gospel to the Gentile Cornelius. Peter had come to understand that the Gospel was for all, not just the Jews.

> *In truth I perceive that God shows no partiality. But in every nation whoever fears Him and works righteousness is accepted by Him. The word which God sent to the children of Israel, preaching peace through Jesus Christ — He is Lord of all — that word you know, which was proclaimed throughout all Judea, and began from Galilee after the baptism which John preached: how God anointed Jesus of Nazareth with the Holy Spirit and with power, who went about doing good and healing all who were oppressed by the devil, for God was with Him. And we are witnesses of all things which He did both in the land of the Jews and in Jerusalem, whom they killed by hanging on a tree. Him God raised up on the third day, and showed Him openly, not to all the people, but to witnesses chosen before by God, even to us who ate and drank with Him after He arose from the dead. And He commanded us to preach to the people, and to testify that it is He who was ordained by God to be Judge of the living and the dead. To Him all the prophets witness that, through His name, whoever believes in Him will receive remission of sins. (Acts 10:34-43)*

In speaking of Jesus, Peter specifically states that Jesus was anointed with the Holy Spirit and power. Peter implies that all Jesus did, doing good, healing, dying on the cross, and being raised from the dead, was done in the power of the Holy Spirit. As Peter was speaking, those gathered in the house of Cornelius received the Holy Spirit. The coming of the Holy Spirit upon those gathered in Cornelius' house was in fulfillment of the promise of Jesus and the emphatic demonstration that the Gentiles were included in the Covenant. The faithful gathered in the upper room, all Jews, had received the Holy Spirit on Pentecost.[155] The same sign, speaking in tongues, that had accompanied the giving of the Spirit to the Jews accompanied the giving of the Spirit to the Gentiles. The coming of the Spirit upon the Church was addressed by Jesus the night that He was betrayed.[156]

Briefly, the Holy Spirit as given to the Church was to abide with the Church, convict men of sin, convict men of righteousness, lead men into truth, and exalt Jesus. Also, the ascended Jesus gives gifts to men. These "Gifts of the Holy Spirit" are intended to enable each member of the Church to minister to every other member. Therefore, dear reader, as God's child you have the same Spirit that enabled Samson to perform his feats of strength, Elijah to outrun chariots, Gideon to obey conquering the Midianites with trumpet and broken pots, Othniel to rise up and be the "ideal" judge, and Jephthah to keep his vow. But, dear reader, you have a great advantage over the Old Testament characters. The Holy Spirit came upon Old Testament people, but He did not abide with them. You, because of the finished work of Jesus, have the indwelling Spirit. You are the "Temple of God" for the Spirit of the Living God indwells you. The Spirit that indwells you has given you a gift or gifts whereby you are to serve the People of God.

> As given to the Church, the Holy Spirit was to abide with the Church, convict men of sin, convict men of righteousness, lead men into truth, and exalt Jesus. Also, the ascended Jesus gives gifts to men.

I beseech you therefore, brethren, by the mercies of God, that you present your bodies a living sacrifice, holy, acceptable to God, which is your reasonable service. And do not be conformed to this world, but be transformed by the renewing of your mind, that you may prove what is that good and acceptable and perfect will of God. For I say, through the grace given to me, to everyone who is among you, not to think of himself more highly than he ought to think, but to think soberly, as God has dealt to each one a measure of faith. For as we have many members in one body, but all the members do not have the same function, so we, being many, are one body in Christ, and individually members of one another.

Having then gifts differing according to the grace that is given to us, let us use them: if prophecy, let us prophesy in proportion to our faith; or ministry, let us use it in our ministering; he who teaches, in teaching; he who exhorts, in exhortation; he who gives, with liberality; he who leads, with diligence; he who shows mercy, with cheerfulness. The service that you are to render is to be sacrificial. (Romans 12:1-8)

Peter addresses these matters, "As each one has received a gift, minister it to one another, as good stewards of the manifold grace of God. If anyone speaks, let him speak as the oracles of God. If anyone ministers, let him do it as with the ability which God supplies, that in all things God may be glorified through Jesus Christ, to whom belong the glory and the dominion forever and ever. Amen."[157] **As the gifted, Spirit-filled people of God, we are empowered by the Spirit of God to serve to glorify Jesus Christ.** As the gifted, Spirit-filled people of God, we are empowered by the Spirit of God to serve to glorify Jesus Christ.

Now let us turn to specifically look at the individual Judges and see how they testify of Jesus and give us hope.

Ask yourself...

- *Am I convinced that the Spirit of the Living God indwells me?*
- *The Spirit is the guarantee of the Life to come. Am I walking by the Spirit and thereby holding the things of this world lightly in my hands?*
- *Having the Spirit of God indwell me means that I am gifted by the Spirit. How are my gifts manifested in the Church? What do I take JOY in doing? What service do I do that never gets old?*
- *Am I ready to give an answer for the Hope that I have? Is my life characterized by hope, joy, the grace of God, and love?*

Here are some action steps you can start with today.

- Write a brief three minute testimony of how God has used you in the Gifts of the Spirit.

- If He has used in various gifts, be ready to share that specific testimony as the Lord leads you.
- As you begin to realize what gives you joy in serving, speak with your Pastor or spiritual leader as to how your gift can be used within your local community and Church.

Chapter 7

THE ROLE OF JUDGES – PART I: OTHNIEL, EHUD, SHAMGAR, AND DEBORAH

And I said to the man who stood at the gate of the year:
'Give me a light that I may tread safely into the unknown'.
And he replied:
'Go out into the darkness and put your hand into the hand of God.
That shall be to you better than light and safer than a known way.

-Minnie Louise Haskins, "God knows"
Quoted by King George VI in a Christmas Broadcast
25 December 1939

Othniel – The Model Judge

The narrative of Othniel's tenure as judge has little more than the essentials to establish him as the ideal.[158] He was raised up by Yahweh to deliver Israel from the oppression of the king of Aram. As the chosen leader, Othniel received Yahweh's spirit, delivered Israel from oppression, and judged Israel for the rest of his life. The land was free from oppression for the remainder of Othniel's life. As the first Judge, Othniel has ties to the Exodus and the Conquest because of his relationship to Caleb. This relationship provides a bridge between the Exodus era and the era of the Judges. As kin and father-in-law, Caleb provides an important link to the Exodus and witnessed the giving of the Law. Yahweh described Caleb as one who "has followed Me fully."[159] He had seen the plagues, participated in the Exodus, witnessed the giving of the Law, and spied out the Promised Land by the time he was forty.[160] He received his inheritance at age eighty-five. As a participant in the Exodus, as spy and conqueror he stands in contrast to the nation: he followed the Lord fully. Othniel was privileged to have Caleb as model and mentor.

Only two events are recorded concerning Othniel's personal life; but, both demonstrate that he followed Caleb's example.[161] Both events are as a result of Caleb's offer to give his daughter, Achsah, as wife to the one who conquered Kiriath-sepher. The first is the capture of the city. The second is his marriage to a woman of his tribe. Capturing Kiriath-sepher is an act attributed to one man. The other military campaigns mentioned in the first chapter of Judges are the efforts of a tribe or a coalition of tribes. Each tribe mentioned, except Simeon, has a measure of failure attributed to its campaign. The failure is stressed by the recurring "did not drive out." For many of the tribes, enslaving the people of the land was more expedient than driving them out.[162] This was a violation of the mandate, "They shall not live in your land, lest they make you sin against Me...."[163]

Othniel is a man in contrast with the predilections of his people.

The mandate of Exodus is repeated in Deuteronomy 7:1-5. The inhabitants of the land were to be smitten, destroyed, and no covenant was to be made with them. The repetition stipulates that the Israelites were not to intermarry. Intermarriage would result in idolatry. Yahweh would then become angry and move against Israel. The failure to drive out the various nations of Canaan, and the expedient practice of enslaving the conquered meant that the Sons of Israel lived among the Canaanites, and they took their daughters for themselves as wives, and gave their own daughters to their sons, and served their gods.[164] Thus the failure to fulfill the mandate in Exodus produced conditions which caused Israel to fail in her covenant obligations.

Othniel is a man in contrast with the predilections of his people. He waged a successful campaign and married a woman from his own tribe. His exemplary personal life provides a suitable backdrop for the pericope containing the elements of the ideal judge. He who is first has all the elements that set him apart as the ideal. Nothing but the essentials are included in the narrative of his judgeship. These essentials provide a skeleton which faintly describe a prophetic role for Othniel: confronting covenantal breach and instruction in covenantal obligation. Since no details are given in Othniel's pericope,[165] conclusions about his prophetic role depend on the summary and the few details we have concerning his personal life.

Othniel, kin to Caleb and son-in-law, is the "model" judge. Being from the tribe of Judah, he foreshadows the fulfillment of Judah's blessing that the scepter shall not depart from Judah, nor a lawgiver from between his feet, until Shiloh comes; and to Him shall be the obedience of the people. Jesus is the fulfillment of the blessing. As Matthew 1 records, sons of Judah ruled in Jerusalem / Judah from David to the Exile. Othniel, as first Judge, points to the One to come who will rule in Israel forever.

Othniel was raised up and sent by Yahweh. Israel was the people of God. Their vocation was to be threefold: God's special treasure, a holy nation, and a kingdom of priests.[166] As the people of God, the Sons of Israel were to be ruled by God. Therefore any man who ruled was to be God's regent. As a consequence, each king was to write his own copy of the law and read that copy all the days of His life.[167] The king and all the people were to be subject to the Law of God. One who set himself upon the throne was a fraud and thus no proper king. Thus, God raised up and sent those who were to rule in Israel. Jesus was sent / raised up by the Father to be the King of kings. Othniel was not king but regent for Yahweh the King.

All who were sent / raised up by Yahweh to rule were empowered by God: Moses in Exodus 3:12; Joshua in Deuteronomy 31:23; Saul and David in 1 Samuel 20:13; and Jereboam in 1 Kings 11:38. To that end, Othniel, as first Judge is the ideal model or "type" of Jesus being from the tribe of Judah, raised up by Yahweh, empowered by Yahweh's Spirit, delivered / saved Israel, brought peace to the land, and married within his tribe. It should be noted that Othniel's name means "Lion of God" further foreshadowing the One who is the "Lion of Judah."

Idolatry led to servitude and oppression. Judges 3:1-2, 4 remind the reader that Israel was being tested, for the generation of the Judges did not know "Yahweh warfare." Yahweh desired to find out if they would obey as their fathers through Moses had been commanded. The Judges, raised up by Yahweh, are representatives of Yahweh who is the true Judge.[168]

Yahweh, through these representatives, exercised His Kingship over the Sons of Israel.

The other heroic figures can rightfully be measured against Othniel the ideal. As the ideal, Othniel anticipates the fulfillment of kingship in Jesus, the Christ. In anticipation of Jesus, Othniel is one who is called savior or deliverer in many English translations.[169] Therefore, each of the other heroic figures anticipated Jesus the Christ in so far as they measure up to the ideal.

As Othniel foreshadows Jesus, we are to imitate Jesus. Paul tells the Corinthian Church that they ought to imitate him as he imitates Christ.[170] Jesus holds Himself as the model after He washes the disciples' feet. "If I then, your Lord and Teacher, have washed your feet, you also ought to wash one another's feet. For I have given you an example, that you should do as I have done to you."[171]

As Othniel foreshadows Jesus, we are to imitate Jesus.

Jesus emphasizes that we are to model Him when He commands the disciples to love one another: "A new commandment I give to you, that you love one another; as I have loved you, that you also love one another. By this all will know that you are My disciples, if you have love for one another."[172] A study of the "even as" clauses is a very fruitful and humbling study for the servant of Jesus who is serious about imitating Jesus. As Othniel was not king but regent for Yahweh the King, so we are to be ambassadors of Christ.

O happy fault, which has deserved to have such and so mighty a Redeemer.
-Missal "Exsultet" on Holy Saturday.

Ehud – The Deliverer Judge

Ehud was raised up by Yahweh to deliver Israel from the dominion of Eglon, king of Moab. Ehud was to take tribute to Eglon, king of Moab. As the bearer of the tribute, Ehud was a messenger from the vassal to the king. The message given was of continued servitude and compliance to Moabite rule. But Ehud had been raised up by Yahweh to deliver the Sons of Israel from oppression. To achieve Yahweh's purpose took careful planning. Ehud had three problems to solve: getting inside the Moabite defenses with a weapon, having an audience alone with the king, and getting away undetected.

Ehud delivered the tribute, but he had been raised up as a deliverer from the obligations manifested in the paying of the tribute. Israel was not to be obligated to Eglon, king of Moab, but to Yahweh. At Gilgal, Ehud turned around and became Yahweh's messenger to the Moabite king, Eglon. This message was not from the oppressed people but from "Elohim, the God of Israel." Ehud was, at this time, Yahweh's prophet to a non-Israelite. Later prophets were used by Yahweh to deliver His word to non-Israelites: Jonah to Ninevah, Elijah to the widow of Zarephath,[173] and Elisha to Hazael.[174]

When Ehud identified the source of the message, he did not use the Covenant name Yahweh because of the concept that the gods of the victor had vanquished the gods of the victim. Since Israel was under the dominion of Moab, Eglon would not have shown respect by standing if Ehud came with a message from Yahweh. Therefore Ehud used language that would elicit respect. Unfortunately for Eglon, the word from *'elohim* terminated his relationship (covenant) with Israel as well as his kingship.

Ehud's work was not yet done.

He had to rally the Sons of Israel to finish the work. His rally cry called for a faith response in the one who had delivered the people from Egypt, for it was Yahweh who gave the Moabites into the hand of Israel.[175] Once again Ehud is a prophetic messenger, calling the people to accept their covenantal relationship and the work that was given as a result. Three times Ehud performs the task of a courier. The first message conveyed is within the context of an illegitimate covenantal relationship which existed because Israel had done evil in the sight of Yahweh. The second message, a word of judgment to a non-Israelite king, placed Ehud in the role of prophet. Lastly, Ehud carries a message to the covenant people. As a prophet of Yahweh, he called them to obedience in faith. Consequently Israel is delivered and rest procured. As Othniel, Ehud is called savior in anticipation of Jesus our Savior.[176]

Not only does Ehud foreshadow Jesus by being called savior, he fore-shadows Jesus as he enters the strong man's house and destroys him. Eglon, as King of Moab represented the pagan gods of Moab. According to the Scriptures, pagan gods are demons.[177] Therefore Eglon is representative of Satan, the strong man, who was destroyed by Jesus.[178] Ehud then gathers the people of God to overthrow the oppressor.

Ehud, being raised up by Yahweh to deliver, foreshadows Jesus and gives us an example. Ehud, who would be considered by the ancient world

> **The same God who raised and empowered Ehud is the same God who has raised you up and empowered you.**

as "odd" because he was left-handed, used what Yahweh had given him in service to Yahweh and Yahweh's people. So too, you are equipped to do what the Lord Christ would have you to do. You are designed for a purpose that glorifies God and serves His people. As the powers of darkness were overcome by Ehud, so too, you are able to resist the devil. Jesus Christ has destroyed the devil so you have a greater advantage over the powers of darkness than Ehud had. The same God who raised and empowered Ehud is the same God who has raised you up and empowered you.

> *But I am poor and needy; Yet Yahweh thinks upon me.*
> *You are my help and my deliverer; Do not delay, O my God.*
> (Psalm 40:17)

Shamgar – Son of Anat

A short pithy narrative gives Shamgar credit for saving Israel.[179] Who was Shamgar? All the other Judges are identified as members of the Sons of Israel by tribe, family or geographical location. Shamgar is said to be the "son of Anat." Anat was a Canaanite goddess of war. It is highly probable that Shamgar was not a member of the Covenant people and therefore is not a "judge" as Othniel and Ehud were. Nevertheless, the text states that Shamgar "delivered" (saved) Israel. A savior in Israel identified with a Canaanite goddess of war is a bit difficult to accept, since the summary specifically attributes the saving activity to Yahweh. Nevertheless, the Old Testament bears witness to Yahweh's use of those outside of Israel to achieve His purposes. Cyrus is called "my Shepherd" and Yahweh's anointed (messiah) in Isaiah 44:28 and Isaiah 45:1. Habakkuk recognized that God was using the Chaldeans for His purposes, and Jonah's shipmates were used to reorient Jonah. Shamgar did not provide rest for the land, but he was apparently in preparation for the work of Deborah.[180]

Though Shamgar is not an Israelite, nevertheless in a limited fashion he foreshadows Christ as he delivers Israel. The deliverance was accomplished singlehandedly and in an unorthodox manner. That Shamgar is not an Israelite may present problems to the casual reader, but God uses whomever He will to achieve His purposes. God used the Empire of Rome to bring Jesus into the World,[181] to crucify Jesus,[182] and to facilitate the spreading of the Gospel.[183] As Shamgar, Cyrus the Chaldean, and Rome were used by God for His purposes, so too, God uses "all things" for our benefit. Let us be alert and

> **Let us be alert and give thanks for God's faithfulness to us even though it means we may have to resolve our lack of understanding and lack of comprehension in the same manner as Habakkuk did.**

give thanks for God's faithfulness to us even though it means we may not understand or comprehend. We must resolve our lack of understanding and lack of comprehension as Habakkuk did: "Yet I will rejoice in the LORD, I will joy in the God of my salvation. The LORD God is my strength; He will make my feet like deer's feet, And He will make me walk on my high hills. "[184]

> *Christian, dost thou see them*
> *On the holy ground,*
> *How the troops of Midian*
> *Prowl and prowl around*
> *Christian, up and smite them,*
> *Counting gain but loss;*
> *Smite them by the merit*
> *Of the Holy Cross*
> -James Mason Neale: "Christian, dost Thou See Them"

Deborah – Prophetess Judge

During the days of Shamgar, the Sons of Israel were living in a society that had nearly come to a standstill. Travel was done circumspectly, peasantry was non-existent, new gods were worshiped,[185] and the Sons of Israel had no ability to go to war.[186] In these dark days, Deborah arose as a prophetess in Israel.[187] As she sat under the Palm tree, the Sons of Israel went to her for judgment. Deborah, as a prophetess and mother in Israel, confronted covenantal breach and taught covenantal obligation. As she sat and judged the Sons of Israel, she is a "second Moses,"[188] a forerunner of Solomon,[189] and a forerunner of the Messiah.[190]

Deborah is similar to Moses in more than the matter of dispensing judgment under a Palm tree. Moses and Deborah have the following similarities: functioned as judges and sat for judgment,[191] the people came to them,[192] proclaimed the word of the Lord,[193] were prophets,[194] pronounced blessings,[195] pronounced curses in the name of the Lord,[196] had military generals,[197] gave instructions to the people as to how the Lord would defeat the enemies,[198] the Lord caused the enemy in chariots to panic and flee,[199] God's victory is told first in prose,[200] then in poetry.[201] Moses had Miriam,[202] and Deborah had Barak[203] to then lead the people in worshiping God after their great deliverance. Therefore Deborah appears as a "second Moses" figure whose authority derives from the God of Sinai. Deborah is not Moses' "equal" but as a "second Moses" figure she foreshadows the "Prophet like you from among their brethren..." spoken of in Deuteronomy 18:18. This prophet like unto Moses was expected by the Jews in the time of Christ, but they had a faulty expectation and failed to see Jesus as the fulfillment of Deuteronomy 18:18.[204]

Deborah is one of two judges identified as a prophet. The second is Samuel. Deborah is one of ten women so designated in the Scriptures. Since Deborah precedes the monarchy, the prophetic office is not a political office. Her activity as a prophetess can best be understood through passages in the Pentateuch dealing with the function and guidelines for prophets.

When Aaron and Miriam spoke against Moses because Moses married a Cushite woman, God answered them by distinguishing Moses from the company of prophets. The prophet would receive communication from the Lord through visions and dreams. Moses had a higher privilege for "with him God spoke mouth to mouth."[205] Some of the ways that God uses to communicate with His prophets are visions, dreams, and dark sayings (riddles). The distinctions between these three means are not clear. Visions seem to be the most restricted having to do with "that which is seen." Dreams are more than the object seen and may have to do with the process as a means of revelation. Dark sayings pertain to subtle enigmatic words like poems or parables. This passage does not indicate whether each prophet was involved in all three activities, but a true prophet of God would receive God's communication in one of these ways.

The message of the prophet is an indication of his veracity. A prophet who performed a sign or wonder which came true was not necessarily a true prophet. If the message of that prophet consisted of "following other gods" then he was to be put to death. On the other hand, if a prophet spoke and the thing did not come to pass, then he was not to be feared. The message and activity of the prophet were both indicators of the prophet's status before God.

Being a prophetess, Deborah was a bearer of God's word to the people. Three times in Judges 4, we have an account of words spoken by her to Barak from the Lord. The first time includes marching orders, a plan of battle, and a promise of victory.[206] In response to Barak's hesitancy, she predicts the honor of victory will go to a woman,[207] and the last word is the attack order.[208] Prior to the account of the battle we are told that she "sent and summoned" Barak. Throughout this account, Deborah's authority over Israel and Barak in particular, is apparent.

Not only is Deborah a prophetess, she also is "the wife of Lappidoth." Deborah being married fits the pattern of all the prophetesses who served Yahweh. It is not a pattern of marriage, but of having a man in her life. Miriam, the sister of Moses, led the women in praise following the crossing of the sea in Exodus 15:20. Huldah, the wife of Shallum the son of Tokhath, the son of Hasrah, keeper of the wardrobe, appears in 2 Kings and 2 Chronicles with regard to one incident. The unnamed prophetess of Isaiah 8:3 is Isaiah's wife. Noahdiah, the prophetess mentioned in Nehemiah 6:14, has no "man in her life" and she is opposed to Nehemiah. Anna, the daughter of Phanuel, appears in Luke 2:36. Philip, the evangelist had four daughters who prophesied.[209] Jezebel, who sought to seduce God's servants, took the label prophetess to herself.[210] The significance of this curious fact depends on the interpreter's prejudice or presupposition. The Scriptures do not lend any support to any interpretation. At the very least, the male figure in each prophetess' life serves to identify the women with the corpus of Israel.

> To call into question Deborah's credentials or qualifications is to cast doubt on the process God used throughout the book of Judges.

Deborah is presented as one judging Israel. The circumstances of her call and establishment of her rule are unknown. We meet her as one whose practice is already established. There is no indication that she usurped a man's position or that she was not the best person for the position. Barak's refusal to go to war without Deborah is a contrast. At this juncture, we do have a woman honored due to a man's failure to accept the role God gave to him. To interpolate the same kind of circumstance into the call and rise of Deborah is unwarranted. The pattern already established in the first three chapters of Judges is for God to raise up a judge to meet a specific crisis. To call into question Deborah's credentials or qualifications is to cast doubt on the process God used throughout the book of Judges.

The Sons of Israel came to Deborah for judgment. This is in contrast to Samuel's circuit. The image of Deborah, seated under a palm tree dispensing judgment calls to mind Solomon. The Sons of Israel came to Deborah as the world came to Solomon.[211] Was her reputation similar to Solomon's? From Judges 5, we get a glimpse of the results of her influence. Prior to Deborah's rise to power, Israel's society had reached a nadir. "The highways were deserted, travelers went by round about ways, the peasantry ceased."[212] Normal commerce, travel, and way of life were disrupted. The situation existed until Deborah "arose as a mother in Israel."[213] A transformation of Israelite society takes place. We do not know how long it took for the society to mobilize. We do know that, under Deborah's leadership, six tribes eventually cooperated in the battle against Sisera.[214]

Can we draw on the image "mother in Israel"? A mother nurtures children. In Deborah's case, the children were the "Sons of Israel." The emphasis she places on the activity of God, recognizing that the battle against Sisera was Yahweh's, leads us to conclude that drawing the people back to Yahweh was central to her nurture of Israel.[215] Barak's willingness to respond, as well as the number of tribes responding, demonstrates a respect and influence such as a mother would have over children.

As a prophetess, she was privileged to be God's spokeswoman in an hour of need. Living in the Old Testament economy, the Holy Spirit did not indwell all the people of God. Consequently, people such as Deborah were highly privileged. But the ideal expressed by Moses is that all God's people would do the work of a prophet.[216] To this end, each member of the Church is indwelt by the Holy Spirit. Any adherent to the true religion, when speaking God's word into another's life is doing the work of a prophet. Such a word should be the "Truth spoken in Love." Such a word should be spoken so that the hearer receives grace and the need of the moment is met.

As a judge, Deborah was divinely gifted to maintain Israel's covenant relationship by calling for inward repentance and providing a defense for external aggression. In judging Israel, she performed the duties of a king. In this capacity she exercised authority over unnumbered men, as the "Sons of Israel" came to her for judgment. To some this may present a problem. Unique in her role as judge, Deborah does not set a pattern or standard for other women unless a woman is gifted as she was. It must be acknowledged that a female authority figure is rare, but that rarity does not preclude any given woman from being given authority by God. As men

To this end, each member of the Church is indwelt by the Holy Spirit. Any adherent to the true religion, when speaking God's word into another's life is doing the work of a prophet. Such a word should be the "Truth spoken in Love." Such a word should be spoken so that the hearer receives grace and the need of the moment is met.

and women seek to minister in this world of woe, we may find that God in His providence has given us examples as well as guidelines which will help us deal with our contemporary issues.

Deborah foreshadows Jesus as she sits under the Palm tree and the Sons of Israel come to her for instructions and adjudication. As prophetess she sits in the shadow of the Prophet who, in His person, was the "Word made flesh," and full of grace and truth. Deborah also foreshadows the fruit of the Gospel in each believer. As the Psalmist writes, "Restore to me the joy of Your salvation, and uphold me by Your generous Spirit. Then I will teach transgressors Your ways, and sinners shall be converted to You." Restoration of Joy will result in others being taught and converted. Deborah, through her instruction, restored the Sons of Israel so that the largest confederation of tribes during the period of the Judges cooperated under her leadership. Let us, male or female, learn to speak the words of God into others' lives in such a manner that the Truth be spoken in love and grace is imparted to the hearer.

The record of the activity of Othniel, Ehud, and Deborah has nothing in the record that would impugn the character of the judge. According to the record, Othniel, Ehud, and Deborah fulfilled all that is said in the pattern and the Sons of Israel enjoyed rest during the lifetime of the Judge.

Ask yourself...

- *Do I speak the words of God into others' lives in such a manner that the Truth is spoken in love and grace is imparted to the hearer?*
- *Am I doing the work of a prophet?*

Here are some action steps you can start with today.

- Reread the accounts of the judges from this chapter.
- What characteristics of each one do you see in your own life?
- Which judge do you most closely resemble?

Chapter 8

THE ROLE OF JUDGES – PART II: GIDEON, TOLAR AND JAIR, JEPHTHAH, IBZAN, ELON, AND ABDON

Faith which does not doubt is dead faith.
-Miguel de Unamuno, La Agonia del Christianismo

Wherever they went out, the hand of Yahweh was against them for calamity, as Yahweh had said, and as Yahweh had sworn to them. And they were greatly distressed. Nevertheless, Yahweh raised up judges who delivered them out of the hand of those who plundered them. Yet they would not listen to their judges, but they played the harlot with other gods, and bowed down to them. They turned quickly from the way in which their fathers walked, in obeying the commandments of Yahweh; they did not do so. And when Yahweh raised up judges for them, Yahweh was with the judge and delivered them out of the hand of their enemies all the days of the judge; for Yahweh was moved to pity by their groaning because of those who oppressed them and harassed them. (Judges 2:15-18)

The pattern in Judges 2 speaks of the rebellion of the Sons of Israel, Yahweh's response, and the result of Yahweh's response. The pattern suggests that Israel's apostasy increases with each passing judge. As Israel's apostasy increases how are the Judges affected?

The record tells us that the land had rest for forty years following Deborah and Barak's victory over Sisera and his army. This period of rest was followed by seven years of oppression by the hand of Midian. Under the oppression of the Midianites, the Sons of Israel were impoverished. As the Sons of Israel had done in the past, they cried out to Yahweh. In response, Yahweh sent a prophet who reminded the Sons of Israel of three things: who Yahweh was (Yahweh was the God of Israel), what Yahweh had done (Yahweh had delivered Israel from Egypt and all the oppressors giving the land to Israel), and the response of the Sons of Israel (Israel failed to listen to Yahweh their God). In being reminded of these three things, the Sons of Israel were faced with Yahweh's faithfulness to the Sinaitic Covenant and their failure in keeping their vow to the Sinaitic Covenant. Following the word of the prophet, the Angel of Yahweh arrives on the scene and addresses Gideon.

Gideon–The Triumph of Yahweh's Mercy and Grace

We are not told how old Gideon was when the Angel of Yahweh speaks to him as he is threshing out his wheat in hiding. But assuming Gideon was an adult by Israelite standards,[217] he had lived at least two thirds of his life in a land enjoying the tranquility of the victory wrought by Deborah, and at most one third of his life under the oppression of Midian. If Gideon was forty-seven, he was born the year Deborah and Barak were victorious. Therefore Gideon would not have seen any of the great victories Yahweh had won as Israel's champion. His only experience was peace followed by severe oppression. His present experience provides no indication that Yahweh is interested in Israel let alone defends and protects His people.

Gideon was hiding out in a wine press as he threshed his wheat. The Angel of Yahweh addresses Gideon with the affirming words, "Yahweh is with you, O valiant warrior." This address appears to be an anomaly for one who hides from the enemy would seem to be anything but valiant. Furthermore, if Yahweh were with Gideon, Gideon ought to be more confident. Gideon's response reveals Gideon's skepticism as well as a healthy bit of doubt. Gideon had heard the tales of: the plundering of Egypt, the flight from Egypt, water supplied in the desert, manna from heaven, clothes that did not wear out, and the various battles. But Gideon sees nothing that would indicate that the Sons of Israel were the people of Yahweh. Given the present oppression by the Midianites and Israel's deep poverty, Gideon had concluded that Yahweh had now abandoned the Sons of Israel.

As it were, the Angel of Yahweh ignores Gideon's skepticism and doubt. Instead of addressing Gideon's disbelief, the Angel of Yahweh turns to Gideon and commands Gideon to go and deliver Israel. The command has three elements: the power available to achieve the action (this your strength), the task to be accomplished (deliver Israel from the Midianites), and the authority of the action (I, that is Yahweh, have sent you). The power available to achieve the action is not vested in Gideon but in Yahweh who is with him as the Angel of Yahweh had announced. The task would be accomplished under the authority of the Covenant King and in the strength of the Covenant King.

The power available to achieve the action is not vested in Gideon but in Yahweh who is with him as the Angel of Yahweh had announced.

Gideon responds with a "reasonable" question pointing out his place in the community. According to the Angel of Yahweh, Gideon will defeat Midian as one man because Yahweh is with him. Gideon, apparently comprehending that he is speaking to Yahweh, asks for a sign. Gideon wants to offer a sacrifice. The sacrifice being accepted reveals to Gideon the one with whom he has been speaking. His skepticism collapses into fear. Yahweh appears to him and grants Gideon peace, Gideon responds by building an altar.

Gideon's first task was to destroy his father's idolatrous shrine.[218] This act parallels the directive that was given to Israel concerning the idols of the land. "Tear down their altars, and smash their sacred pillars, and hew down their Asherim, and burn their graven images with fire."[219] Gideon was not directed to tear down a Canaanite shrine, but his own father's shrine. Israel was involved in the Canaanite abomination. This incident demonstrated that Gideon was to be Israel's savior and that the gods of the Midianites were unable to contend against the God of Israel. The "Baal" that Gideon had torn down was unable to contend for himself for "Baal" was no god.

Gideon then had his primary task before him: defeat the Midianites in battle and deliver Israel. Encouragement and affirmation were given through the sign of the fleece and dew.[220] Gideon raised an army according to Yahweh's instructions following the gracious fulfillment of Gideon's requests.[221] Under Yahweh's direction, the army is reduced to only three hundred. Their weapons were to be pitchers, torches, and voices. Dependency on Yahweh was emphasized. The Midianites fought one another as Yahweh "set every man's sword against his companion."[222] The victory was not brought about by military might or military activity. The victory was won because the word of Yahweh was acting through Gideon who was placed in a prophetic role.

Following his victory over the Midianites, Gideon returned to punish Succoth and Penuel because they had refused him aid.[223] This act was not an act of deliverance but was vengeful. Gideon had been raised up by Yahweh to deliver Israel from the hand of Midian. That task had been completed. Instead of singing a song of praise as Deborah and Barak did,[224] he punished those who had refused to help. Deborah and Barak acknowledged those who had refused to help,[225] but there was no hostility toward those who did not participate.

The Sons of Israel asked Gideon to be their king after his victory over Midian was secure.[226] He properly refused saying, "Yahweh shall rule over you." But the act that followed belied his submission to Yahweh, for he built an ephod from the spoils of war that led to idolatry,[227] and named his son, by his Shechemite concubine, Abimelech, which means "My father is king." Gideon is the last Judge of whom it was said that the land was undisturbed as a result of his activity.

Gideon's tenure as judge is characterized by destruction. His destruction of his father's shrine was a confrontation with covenantal abrogation, the destruction of his own and the Midianites involved instruction in covenantal obligation. These events took place under Yahweh's watchful eye and were prophetic in nature. Yahweh had raised Gideon up to "deliver Israel from the hand of Midian."[228] The destruction of his father's shrine authenticated him as a leader designated by Yahweh to bring about deliverance. The destruction of his army made it impossible for anyone except Yahweh to receive glory for the ultimate victory. The destruction of Midian was the fulfillment of his commission to deliver Israel from Midian's oppression. But Gideon did some destroying on his own and not under Yahweh's watchful eye. He destroyed Penuel and Succoth because they had refused to give him aid. His last destructive act was the undoing of all religious reformation that may have been accomplished under his administration. He built an ephod that became an idol in Israel.

The record of Gideon's exploits places Gideon as a forerunner of Christ in at least four ways. Gideon is sent by Yahweh to deliver the people from oppression. Gideon is empowered by the Spirit of God to bring about the victory.[229] Gideon defeats the oppressor in a manner that brings glory to God and God alone.[230] When offered the kingship, Gideon refuses, stating that Yahweh was to rule over Israel.[231] Thus Gideon acknowledges the Kingship of Yahweh, clearly established at Sinai and as the rule of Moses and Joshua implied. Gideon brings peace to the land for forty years.[232]

Gideon is not only a forerunner of Christ, he is also very much an example of the triumph of Yahweh's mercy and grace in the presence of human weakness, inability, and unbelief. When the Angel of Yahweh confronts Gideon in the wine press, Gideon is an unbelieving skeptic convinced that Yahweh has abandoned Israel. Yet this unbelieving skeptic is listed as one of the "heroes of faith."[233] The skeptic in the wine press asks for **Gideon, weak in faith, is an example of Yahweh answering the prayer, "Lord, I believe; help my unbelief!"** three signs to confirm his call and task. Furthermore, Yahweh, knowing the weakness of Gideon's faith gives Gideon a fourth sign. Yahweh sent Gideon down to the Midianite camp where he heard a man relating a dream that confirmed that Yahweh had given the Midianites into the hand of Gideon. Gideon, weak in faith, is an example of Yahweh answering the prayer, "Lord, I believe; help my unbelief!"

Gideon is also an example of the dangers of success. Gideon had won a great victory. It was such a great victory that it becomes a reference point for the Psalmist[234] and Isaiah.[235] The victory had been won because Yahweh had sent Gideon and was with Gideon. But Gideon apparently forgot who was to receive the glory. As a consequence, Gideon led Israel back into idolatry. Gideon, even though he acknowledged that he and his son would not rule, belied his acknowledgment as he gathered the wealth of the people to make an ephod and named his son Abimelech (my father is king).

No judge after Gideon is said to bring rest to the land. Yahweh refuses to deliver the people from oppression saying, "Go and cry out to the gods which you have chosen."[236] Subsequent to these words of Yahweh, no judge brings deliverance. Jephthah only partially delivers Israel from their oppressors. The structure of the book itself seems to change as the character of the judges change.

Dear reader, before we leave Gideon consider the shadow of the saint in this narrative. The weapons of warfare were trumpets, empty pitchers, torches, and voices. The torches were placed in the empty pitchers. At the appointed time the pitchers were broken, trumpets blown, torches held high, and a loud shout of the sword of Yahweh and of Gideon. Where is the shadow of the saint? The clay pot! We are to be broken vessels. The Holy Spirit indwells each believer. But the Holy Spirit cannot "shine" in and through us until we are broken. Also, what is the sword that we are given? The sword for us is the Word of God which is able to divide between the thought and intentions of the heart.

> *Whoever has lived long enough to find out what life is,*
> *knows how deep a debt of gratitude we owe to Adam,*
> *the first great benefactor of our race,*
> *he brought death into the world.*
> -Mark Twain in Pudd'nhead Wilson chapter three.

Abimelech and Jotham – The Bramble Bush Fable

Gideon's forty years of rest were followed by great strife brought about by the one leader of the judge era who lies outside the bounds of the covenant. The author of Judges says that Abimelech was made king[237] and "held sway over Israel for three years." His rise to power and his end are recorded in Judges 9. Yahweh, the covenant name, is conspicuously absent from this chapter. But He appears three times under another name.[238] Abimelech's rise to power was not preceded by a period of oppression, nor was it brought about because of the activity of Yahweh. His coming to power was not motivated by a need for deliverance and did not result in a period of tranquility. Abimelech's rule was outside the pattern established by Yahweh in Judges 2.

Abimelech's rise to power was brought about through conspiracy and murder.[239] The conspiracy was based upon his family ties to Shechem and his inheritance from his father Gideon. To secure his inheritance he hired a band of ruffians and murdered his brothers, the competition. Other claimants having been removed, Abimelech was made king. The local rulers gave his authority to him. The end to his government came violently in a civil conflict.[240] An evil spirit sent from God divided Abimelech from his power base, the men of Shechem.[241] Civil strife ensued bringing about a fulfillment of the curse uttered by Jotham.[242] The curse was given as part of a fable and commentary enunciated in conjunction with Abimelech's coronation day.[243]

Jotham's Fable: The trees were looking for one of their own kind to rule over them. Who is the king of the trees? Why would the trees look for a king? The olive tree, fig tree, and the vine understood who they were and what they were to be doing. The olive tree and the vine even went so far as to say that God and men benefited from their fruit. These three understood that to "wave over the trees" would necessitate leaving their appointed obligations to take on that which was not theirs to do. Having been rejected by the olive, fig, and vine, the trees went to the bramble. The bramble, by its nature, is but a plant to be torn up and discarded for it produces nothing to honor God or men. When the bramble was asked to be king, the bramble replied conditionally. The phrase "if in truth"[244] connects the fable to the coronation of Abimelech. If the trees were approaching the bramble sincerely, its rule (shade) was available. If the approach was not "in truth" destruction would follow.

Abimelech's rise to power was not in truth; therefore, the bramble's response becomes a curse. King Abimelech and a monarchy in general is a humanistic alternative to the ideal: Yahweh the Covenant King. The humanistic alternative could not offer the conditions that would produce a tranquil state for the community of Israel. Even though the elements of the ideal ruler are missing in Judges 9 and Abimelech is presented as a humanistic alternative to Yahweh's design, the covenant Yahweh made with Israel cast a long shadow over the narrative. Shechem was an important city in the life of Israel. At this place Yahweh appeared to Abram and Abram built an altar to Yahweh.[245] Jacob bought a parcel of ground and erected an altar in the region.[246] Jacob also purified his household and buried "strange gods" near Shechem.[247] But the most important events in the life of the nation that took place at Shechem were the covenant renewals under Joshua.[248]

Following the destruction of Ai, Joshua had an altar of uncut stones built according to the command of Moses.[249] The people were then arranged on Mount Ebal and Mount Gerizim for a reading of the Law: the blessing and the curse.[250] The second covenant renewal preceded Joshua's death.[251] Joshua reviewed Israel's history in terms of the acts of Yahweh. Following the recapitulation, Joshua charged the people and they responded with an oath of fidelity to Yahweh.[252] A stone was set up as a witness and Joshua wrote the statute and ordinance in the book of the Law. Shechem was also one of the cities of refuge[253] and given to the Kohathites.[254]

With such a rich heritage, it would seem anomalous to find that *Baal–berith* (lord of the covenant), not Yahweh, was the god worshiped in Shechem. Yet if the tendency of Israel is examined, *Baal–berith* is not an anomaly but a natural occurrence in disobedient Israel. The people held a false conception of Yahweh. Yahweh had become a Baal, the same type of god that their neighbors worshiped. As a result sacrifice and ritual were deemed more important than proper moral conduct. Thus the word of Yahweh through Amos explicitly decries festivals, assemblies, and sacrifice.[255] Yahweh desired justice and righteousness. Jeremiah suggests that the people were not conscious of forsaking Yahweh.[256] Israel's tendency to make Yahweh in the image of their neighbor's gods would produce *Baal–berith* in Shechem: a Canaanite version of the God to whom Israel swore allegiance in the last days of Joshua.

Jotham further accentuates the perversion represented by the existence of Baal–berith. When he was told of Abimelech's coronation, he went to the top of Mount Gerizim and addressed the people from there. Mount Gerizim was to be the mountain of blessing. Mount Ebal was to be the mountain of cursing.[257] If the men of Shechem had acted in good faith with the family of Gideon, then they would have been able to rejoice in Abimelech their king and Jotham's words may have been a blessing.[258] But Abimelech's coronation was covered with the blood of Jotham's brothers. Thus Jotham uttered a curse from the mountain of blessing.

The curse from the mountain of blessing was fulfilled through the intervention of God.[259] God sent the spirit that divided Abimelech from the men of Shechem. It is God who is given credit for repaying Abimelech and the Shechemites for their treachery. If God is understood as a term describing Yahweh, then once again Yahweh intervenes to extricate Israel. The pattern outlined in Judges 2:11-19 stipulates that Yahweh raised up judges to deliver Israel from oppression. Abimelech's government did not follow a foreign oppression, but arose during an apostate situation in Israel. Consequently no deliverance was necessary, and no rest was procured. As a result, Judges 9 is a record of how things are when Israel was ruled according to the pattern of other nations and forsaking Yahweh who was to be Israel's king.

Withing Judges 9, Jotham foreshadows Jesus as he confronts covenant abrogation, standing against Abimelech's usurpation of power and confronting the people with the nature of kingship as represented in the person of Abimelech. Jotham was not heard in the same manner as succeeding prophets and Jesus were not heard.

> **We must remember, "greater is He that is in you than he that is in the world."**

The ensuing events of the chapter vindicate Jotham and reveal Abimelech as a self-serving monarch who led the people away from their covenant obligation.

Dear reader, the Shechemites traded Yahweh, the Covenant King, for Baal – berith, lord of the covenant. They kept the shell and gave up the substance. Not willing to accept Yahweh on Yahweh's terms, they made Yahweh after their own mind / terms. The Shechemites were ungodly, doing ungodly things in an ungodly way. We are prone to do the same. Often we find that it is inconvenient, painful, or lonely to obey God's word so we compromise. We want to "get along," so we "fudge" and do not do what we know we ought. Let us be courageous, as Jotham, and confront those that stray from the Truth. We must remember that "greater is He that is in you than he that is in the world."

> *My sword, I give to him that shall succeed me in my pilgrimage, and my courage and skill to him that can get it.–Mr. Valiant for Truth (John Bunyan in Pilgrim's Progress, pt. 2)*

Tolar and Jair – Witnesses of God's Faithfulness

Following Abimelech we are introduced to Tola and Jair. The record tells us very little of either, but both are said to have judged Israel. Tola is said to have saved Israel. This places him in the company of Othniel, Ehud, and Shamgar. Jair is said to have had thirty sons who rode on thirty donkeys and they had thirty cities. It can be concluded that Jair behaved like a king and his rule was characterized by peace. These two conclusions are based upon the sons and cities. As Jesus entered into Jerusalem riding on a donkey signifying that He came in peace, so too, Jair's sons riding on donkeys may indicate that Jair's rule was peaceful. The multitude of cities speaks for themselves since they were called "Havvoth-Jair" (the towns of Jair).

Both Tola and Jair are witness to Yahweh's faithfulness. Those who were to follow Yahweh had done great wickedness by redefining Yahweh and crowning their own king. Yet Yahweh was faithful in spite of the Covenant breakers' wickedness, for Yahweh raised up one to deliver after Abimelech died. Following the deliver's death, Yahweh raised up another to judge. Both Tola and Jair foreshadow Jesus, however faintly, for they bear witness of Yahweh's Covenant faithfulness which culminates in the person and work of Jesus.

Following the death of Jair, the Sons of Israel forsake Yahweh and serve other gods. Yahweh gives the Sons of Israel into the hands of the Ammonites and Philistines. Once again the Israelites were crushed. Once again they called upon Yahweh and confessed their sin. Yahweh reiterated the various oppressors from whom the Israelites had been delivered. Having reminded Israel of these deliverances, Yahweh tells Israel to cry out to the gods they have chosen. Yahweh says, "Therefore I will deliver you no more."[260] This is reminiscent of the conversation Yahweh has with Moses in Exodus 32:9-10, "I have seen this people, and indeed it is a stiff-necked people! Now therefore, let Me alone, that My wrath may burn hot against them and I may consume them. And I will make of you a great nation …." Moses pleads for the nation on the basis of Yahweh's character and the Covenant made with Abraham, Isaac, and Jacob. Here in Judges, Yahweh's character and Covenant are "at risk." Following Yahweh's exhortation to go to the other gods, Israel not only cries for help but repents. The foreign gods were put away and Yahweh was served.

Once again the Covenant King pursues His Covenant people. It is axiomatic that Yahweh disciplines His wayward people. As the writer to the Hebrews says as he quotes Proverbs, "And you have forgotten the exhortation which speaks to you as to sons: 'My son, do not despise the chastening of the LORD, Nor be discouraged when you are rebuked by Him; For whom the LORD loves He chastens, And scourges every son whom He receives.'"[261] Here in Judges 10, the Covenant people were drawn by their Covenant King to repent and serve Him. Yahweh's faithfulness is not only attested to by Tola and Jair, but also the discipline that leads to repentance bears witness to His faithfulness.

Once again the Covenant King pursues His Covenant people. It is axiomatic that Yahweh disciplines His wayward people.

> *Constantly speak the truth, boldly rebuke vice,*
> *and patiently suffer for the Truth's sake.*
> "The Book of Common Prayer," St. John the Baptist's Day

Jephthah The Soldier Judge

As the Sons of Ammon gathered and the Sons of Israel gathered in response, the recurring issue of leadership had to be addressed. In Judges 1:1, the Sons of Israel asked Yahweh who should lead them. Here in Judges 10:18, the leaders of Gilead inquire among themselves. The elders of Gilead turn to a brigand who had been driven out of their midst.[262] Jephthah was a professional soldier, accustomed to leading men and warring. Through a protracted negotiation, Jephthah was accepted as head in Gilead. He was first offered a position as chief in Gilead. Jephthah wanted more control, so he was made head.

When the elders and Jephthah agreed on an arrangement, Yahweh was called in as witness.[263] The compact was ratified at the local sanctuary. The word which Jephthah spoke before Yahweh at Mizpah may have been an oath of office. Even though Yahweh did not raise Jephthah up, his assumption of duties was a matter done in the presence of Yahweh.

As the head of the Gileadites, Jephthah enters into negotiations with the Ammonites. Ammon contended that Israel had taken land from them.[264] They wanted that land returned. Jephthah rejected their claim

85

on historical and theological grounds. The Ammonites were not present when Israel entered the land. Yahweh gave them the land even as the land that Ammon possessed had been given to them by their god Chemosh. These negotiations broke off. Jephthah called Yahweh in as judge to determine who was right.

With negotiations broken off, there was no alternative but to go to war. At this juncture the text states that Yahweh's spirit came upon Jephthah.[265] This would indicate that the battle was another in which the victory was not brought about by military might or activity, but by the power of Yahweh. Consequently Jephthah is placed in a prophetic role: endowed with the spirit of Yahweh and leading the people to overthrow oppression that was the result of covenant abrogation. Yahweh gave the Ammonites to Jephthah.[266]

Jephthah made one other deal. This last deal was a hasty vow prior to battle.[267] This vow is in stark contrast to the negotiations made with the elders of Gilead and with the Ammonites. Its haste seems incongruous when placed next to Jephthah's solemn oath at Mizpah. Yet the vow was made. Jephthah was careful to fulfill this vow. Jephthah did not bring rest to the land nor did he deliver Israel from her oppressors. Prior to Jephthah's judgeship Yahweh had said, "I will deliver you no more."[268] Israel was oppressed by the Philistines and the Ammonites.[269] Jephthah delivered Israel from the hand of the Ammonites but not the Philistines. The Philistines would be a problem for Israel until the time of David.[270]

> **One who abides with Yahweh must be one who keeps his word.**

The solemn oath at Mizpah and the hasty vow made prior to battle set Jephthah apart from the Sons of Israel. The Sons of Israel had said, "All that the LORD has said we will do, and be obedient."[271] At the various Covenant Renewals this commitment was reaffirmed, but Israel consistently broke the Covenant. Jephthah made and kept his oaths. This is a foreshadowing of Jesus. You may be aghast, appalled, horrified or incredulous that Jephthah kept his hasty vow of Judges 11:30-31, but consider Psalm 15. The Psalmist asks, "Yahweh, who may abide in Your tabernacle? Who may dwell in Your holy hill?" The answer to these questions includes, "He who swears to his own hurt and does not change." One who abides with Yahweh must be one who keeps his word. For those who live with Yahweh are to share Yahweh's character. As the New Testament tells us,

"...let God be true but every man a liar..." Yahweh is called the God of Truth.[272]

As we consider Psalm 15, we ought also to consider Ecclesiastes 5:1-6. Specifically verses four and five which say, "When you make a vow to God, do not delay to pay it; For He has no pleasure in fools. Pay what you have vowed — Better not to vow than to vow and not pay." Note that there is no allowance for foolish or hasty vows. All vows are to be paid.

Jesus addresses the issue of fulfilling your word with the exhortation that our "...Yes be Yes and ...No be No. For whatever is more than these is from the evil one."[273] James also addresses this issue.

> *Come now, you who say, "Today or tomorrow we will go to such and such a city, spend a year there, buy and sell, and make a profit;" whereas you do not know what will happen tomorrow. For what is your life? It is even a vapor that appears for a little time and then vanishes away. Instead you ought to say, "If the Lord wills, we shall do this or that." But now you boast in your arrogance. All such boasting is evil." (James 4:13-16)*

Therefore, Jephthah, as painful as the fulfillment of his hasty vow was, kept his word. Thus Jephthah modeled Yahweh who is faithful to His Word. In keeping his vow, Jephthah foreshadows Jesus who "endured the cross" that we may have life.

Unlimited power is apt to corrupt the minds who possess it.
-William Pitt, Earl of Chatham, House of Lords, 9 January 1770

Ibzan, Elon, and Abdon – Minor Judges

Following Jephthah, the Book of Judges presents three more Judges of whom little is said. All three are said to have judged Israel therefore they are to be regarded among those who Yahweh raised up to deliver the Sons of Israel from an oppressor. Once again the faithfulness of Yahweh is demonstrated. It can be presumed that all that was true of previous judges is true for these three.

The record of Ibzan lets us see dimly how the judges themselves were becoming corrupt. Ibzan gave his daughters in marriage and brought in women from elsewhere for his sons. You ask, "How is this evidence for Ibzan's corruption?" Yahweh had specifically charged the Sons of Israel not to give their daughters in marriage to the Canaanites nor to take women from the Canaanites for their sons.[274] Since the text makes no mention of any affiliation with the Sons of Israel and uses the term "elsewhere," it can be presumed that Ibzan was guilty of marrying his children with those outside the Sons of Israel.

Nothing can be said about Elon other than his time as judge was evidence of Yahweh's continual faithfulness to a "stiff-necked" people. Abdon, like Jair, behaved like a king having his sons and grandsons riding on donkeys. The Judges were not to be kings but serve the Covenant King, Yahweh. Therefore Jair and Abdon speak to the corruption of the judges.

> **Since the outstanding characteristic of Jephthah was his faithfulness to his oath the text highlights the faithfulness of Yahweh by placing Tola and Jair prior to Jephthah and Ibzan, Elon, and Abdon after.**

In review, Tola, Jair, Ibzan, Elon, and Abdon are said to have judged Israel but very little information is given about them.[275] Each of these five judges are identified as members of the Sons of Israel by tribe, town or geographical location. Since all are credited with judging Israel we can assume that each of them were: raised up by Yahweh, empowered by Yahweh, and performed some act of deliverance.[276] Yet only one, Tola, is said to have saved Israel. Tola and Jair judge Israel after Abimelech dies and prior to the oppression that lead to the raising up of Jephthah. Ibzan, Elon, and Abdon follow Jephthah and precede Samson. I suggest that these five are on either side of Jephthah to highlight Yahweh's faithfulness. Since the outstanding characteristic of Jephthah was his faithfulness to his oath, the text highlights the faithfulness of Yahweh by placing Tola and Jair prior to Jephthah and Ibzan, Elon, and Abdon after.

Following the death of Jair, Yahweh gave the Sons of Israel into the hands of the Philistines and the sons of Ammon. The Philistines and Ammonites shattered and crushed the Sons of Israel on the eastern side of the Jordan. Ammon crossed the Jordan causing great distress among the tribes West of Jordan. When the Sons of Israel cried out to Yahweh,

Yahweh reiterates the various times He had delivered them. Yet they had forsaken Yahweh and served other gods. Therefore Yahweh tells them, "Go and cry out to the gods which you have chosen; let them deliver you in your time of distress." The Philistines were to plague Israel until the time of David. Thus the Sons of Israel were not delivered from the Philistines during the days of the Judges.

The book of Judges deals with the leadership gap in Israel that existed when Joshua died.[277] This leadership vacancy plagues Israel at the end of the book.[278] Between the first and last verses the author has given us a record of those whom Yahweh raised up as leaders. The author provided a pattern establishing the need for leadership and criteria for the ideal leaders.[279] The first few judges approximate the ideal very closely, bringing rest to the land. With the passing of Gideon there are some radical changes in the book.

Israel is not unless Yahweh calls it into being and sustains it throughout history.

The book of Judges forms part of a consistent narrative with the narratives preceding and following. Israel, in spite of its failure to keep the Covenant, is dependent on Yahweh for its very existence. The judge, raised up by Yahweh, is, by his very existence, an indictment of Israel's apostasy against the most basic demand of the law to have "no other gods before Me." Within the structure of the book, the death notice of each judge serves to remind the reader that Israel's apostasy has increased.

Israel is not unless Yahweh calls it into being and sustains it throughout history. The book of Judges, probably written or at least edited during the exile[280] bears witness to Yahweh's commitment to the Covenant and the Covenant people during a very dark period in the nation's life. Therefore the Book of Judges was written/edited to give hope to an exiled people who had lost all that they held as identifying them as a people: Temple, Priesthood, Kings, Jerusalem, and the Promised Land.

It is difficult to attribute any specific foreshadowing of Jesus with any of the five. But Yahweh's faithfulness to His Covenant is ultimately fulfilled in Jesus. Our faithful God may seem to be far away as we go through valleys of death. The Book of Judges is a national descent into a deep valley of death. Yet throughout the Book, the great Shepherd of the sheep intervenes protecting, calling His people back to Himself, and maintaining His Covenant relationship in spite of the nation's rebellion.

As you go through "valleys of death," do you see the evidence of the One who loved you and died for you? Each day is a testimony of His faithfulness as are the seasons of the year or the rainbow after a rain. The One who sustained Israel during the dark days of the Judges will sustain you through the dark days of your life. May I remind you that the writer in the midst of the sorrow and pain of Lamentations says, "This I recall to my mind, therefore I have hope. Through Yahweh's mercies we are not consumed, because His compassions fail not. They are new every morning; great is Your faithfulness. 'Yahweh is my portion,' says my soul, 'Therefore I hope in Him!'"[281] Yahweh's compassions and faithfulness are daily demonstrated, at the very least, in the rhythms of nature: day and night, the four seasons, and the bow in the cloud.[282] In your darkest days of doubt and unbelief look to the daily evidence of our God's compassion and faithfulness and know that, as Jephthah kept his vow, so too, God is faithful to His word.[283]

> **The Book of Judges is a national descent into a deep valley of death. Yet throughout the Book, the great Shepherd of the sheep intervenes protecting, calling His people back to Himself, and maintaining His Covenant relationship in spite of the nation's rebellion.**

Ask yourself...

- *Is the Holy Spirit able to "shine" in and through me?*
- *What is the sword that I have been given to win the battles I face in my life?*
- *Do I find it inconvenient, painful or lonely to obey God's word?*
- *Do I compromise because I want to "get along" and do not do what I know I ought?*
- *How have I experienced the Lord's faithfulness?*
- *Have I ever behaved in a godless fashion as the Shechemites?*
- *Has God's mercy and discipline drawn me back to Him?*
- *Do I keep my word?*
- *Do I model the God that I profess to serve?*

- *As I go through "valleys of death," do you see the evidence of the One who loved and died for me?*

Here are some action steps you can start with today.

- Be courageous, as Jotham, and confront those that stray from the Truth.
- Remember that "greater is He that is in you than he that is in the world."
- If you are not enjoying fellowship with God, honestly evaluate if you are involved in a godless fashion and repent and ask for God's mercy and grace.
- If there is a promise or vow you have made that you have not fulfilled, do it today.
- In your darkest days of doubt and unbelief look to the daily evidence of our God's compassion and faithfulness and know that, as Jephthah kept his vow, so too God is faithful to His word. Read Psalm 118.

Chapter 9

THE ROLE OF JUDGES – PART III:
SAMSON, ELI, AND SAMUEL

> *Be a sinner and sin strongly,*
> *but more strongly have faith and rejoice in Christ.*
> -Martin Luther in "Letter to Melanchthon"

Samson–Epitome of Israel

The last Judge in the Book of Judges is Samson. We have more information about Samson than we have of any other Judge. We have the record of his birth and we are told how he dies. We have only death notices for the other judges. Samson was unique among the judges. He was set apart as a Nazarite prior to his birth. His position as a Nazarite meant that he was consecrated to Yahweh. It could be argued that all the judges were set apart / consecrated for the purpose of delivering Israel from oppression, but Samson's status as a Nazarite set him apart for a particular manner of living. His calling entailed upon him a lifestyle that would confront a people comfortable with their Philistine overlords.[284]

He did not lead the Sons of Israel into battle. His battles were personal vendettas. Each vendetta arose from an incident involving a woman. Judges 14-15 records a series of events that arose from Samson's desire to marry a woman of Timnah. His parents, as good Israelite parents, counseled against marrying the woman of Timnah, but they did not know that Yahweh was seeking an occasion against the Philistines.[285] Four events take place as a result of Samson's desire. Prior to three of the events the text explicitly states that Yahweh's spirit empowered Samson.[286] These four events are followed by two encounters with women and events resulting from those encounters conclude the Samson narrative.[287] The bulk of the material pertains to Delilah's entrapment of Samson and the Philistine joy at Samson's ultimate capture. The first four events close with Samson calling upon Yahweh, Yahweh answering, and the observation that Samson judged Israel for twenty years.[288]

According to the record, Samson was an immoral man who was: a Nazarite empowered by Yahweh, judged Yahweh's people, called upon Yahweh in time of trouble, and was answered. He broke his Nazarite vow and failed to comply with the directive not to marry Canaanite women. His personal life is the antithesis of Othniel's.

Samson was raised up by Yahweh to "begin to deliver Israel from the hands of the Philistines."[289] Therefore his activity as a judge has a smaller scope than the other judges who had been raised up to deliver the Sons of Israel from their oppressor.[290] The events arising out of Samson's desire for the woman of Timnah should be understood as the battle narrative marking the beginning of his judgeship and corresponding to the battle narratives of other judges. Since Samson was only to begin to bring about deliverance, the escapade in Gaza could possibly be a vignette describing Samson's ongoing conflict during his twenty-year rule. His whole life would then be marked by continual conflict with the oppressor. During his tenure as judge, he continually confronted Israel's covenantal failure in his person. His uncut hair was a mute, passive testimony to abrogation and obligation. Yahweh left Samson when this one witness was destroyed. Samson understood the significance of his hair for he is slow to disclose his secret to Delilah, and when he does, she knows by his manner that she possessed the great secret.[291] He early broke his Nazarite vow, but the visible manifestation of that vow was mute testimony to his obligations as well as the nation's.

Samson epitomizes the nation of Israel and prefigures Jesus.

If Gideon's judgeship was a significant turning point because it marked the beginning of the decline of the judges, then Samson's judgeship is the nadir. Samson epitomizes the nation of Israel and prefigures Jesus. As is outlined in the pattern given to us in Judges 2, the Book of Judges presents the theme of Israel's recurring rebellion, Yahweh's discipline, Israel's crying out to Yahweh, and Yahweh sending a deliverer resulting in a period of peace.

Samson epitomizes the nation in at least five ways:

Set Apart. As Samson was set apart for Yahweh's service prior to birth, so too, Israel was set apart as His peculiar people prior to their birth as a nation. When did Israel become a Nation? They became a nation at Sinai as they were given the Law that would define them as Yahweh's possession, a Royal Priesthood, and a holy nation. Prior to being given that Law, they were set apart from all other nations as a consequence of the Abrahamic Covenant.

A Peculiar Relationship with Yahweh. Samson and the Sons of Israel broke the Covenant that bound them to Yahweh, yet maintained an understanding that they had a peculiar relationship with Yahweh. Samson, as a Nazarite, was to "... separate himself from wine and similar drink; ... eat nothing that is produced by the grapevine, from seed to skin. ... no razor shall come upon his head; until the days are fulfilled for which he separated himself to the LORD, he shall be holy. Then he shall let the locks of the hair of his head grow. ...not go near a dead body." Samson violated the third element of the Nazarite vow by: killing the lion and taking honey from its carcass, killing the thirty in Ashkelon, and the thousand in Lehi. The text does not specifically say that Samson violated the first element of eating and/or drinking the produce of the vine; but, given the information about the feast in Judges 14 and the information revealed in chapter 16, it can be assumed that Samson violated this element also. Yet Samson maintained a commitment to the Nazarite vow by letting the locks of his hair grow. He acknowledges this as he confesses to Delilah, "No razor has ever come upon my head, for I have been a Nazarite to God from my mother's womb. If I am shaven, then my strength will leave me, and I shall become weak, and be like any other man."

In like manner, the Sons of Israel violated the Sinaitic Covenant yet maintained an understanding that they were consecrated to Yahweh. This is evident in the name of the god of Shechem Baal – Berith. It is also evident as the Sons of Israel cry out to Yahweh in their despair. But as Samson misunderstood the relationship of his hair to the Nazarite vow, so too, Israel misunderstood the Covenant relationship they had with Yahweh. Samson understood that cutting his hair would result in him becoming weak, but "he did not know that Yahweh had departed from him." In like manner the Sons of Israel in the days of Jeremiah understood that the Temple and Jerusalem were the place of Yahweh's dwelling among them, but they too did not know when Yahweh had departed.

God's Instrument of Power. Samson was not able to perform his feats of strength in his own strength. Samson was the instrument Yahweh used to demonstrate His power and faithfulness among the Sons of Israel. There are seven feats of great strength attributed to Samson. They are: killing a lion with his bare hands, killing thirty men, catching three hundred foxes and turning them loose in the Philistine's fields, striking an unknown number to avenge his wife, killing a thousand with the jawbone of a donkey, carrying the gates of Gaza uphill toward Hebron, and pushing the pillars of the house apart so that the house was destroyed and many died. The text states that the Spirit of Yahweh came upon Samson prior to killing the lion, killing the thirty in Ashkelon, and killing the thousand in Lehi. Prior to his last feat of strength, Samson prays, "O Lord GOD, remember me, I pray! Strengthen me, I pray, just this once, O God, that I may, with one blow, take vengeance on the Philistines for my two eyes!"[292]

Samson had come to understand that it was not the hair, but Yahweh who gave him strength. So too, throughout Israel's history, Yahweh's strength not Israel's was the means used to deliver Israel from their oppressors. This was manifested throughout Israel's history beginning with Egypt, continuing through Joshua and Judges, and ultimately culminating in the New Heavens and New Earth. As part of the Covenant made at Sinai, Yahweh was committed to Israel's defense and protection therefore Israel was not to make foreign alliances but to trust Yahweh alone.[293]

Moral Failure. Throughout the Old Testament adultery and fornication are terms used to describe apostasy and idolatry. Therefore Samson's moral issues with women epitomize Israel's covenant failure as they served the Baals and Asherahs.

Desperation for God. Following the confrontation at Lehi, Samson cried out to Yahweh thinking that he would die of thirst. His prayer was answered as God caused water to flow from the rock and Samson was revived. This event in Samson's life is for Samson as it was for Israel in the desert.[294] Samson calls out to Yahweh at the end of his life. Having given up the one piece of the Nazarite vow that he valued all his life, Samson becomes a spectacle for the Philistines. Samson endured until the opportunity arose that enabled him to avenge his eyes. Samson had learned the lesson that whatever strength he had was given to him from Yahweh, so he prays and asks for strength. Samson's ordeal as a spectacle for the Philistines and his turning to Yahweh is a foreshadowing of the ordeal of Judah in Babylon as expressed by Psalm 137.

Samson prefigures Jesus in at least five ways:

- *Samson's birth announcement prefigures Jesus' birth announcement. Both births were announced to the mother by a messenger from Heaven.*
- *The Sons of Israel rejected the leadership of Samson as they rejected Jesus.*
- *As Samson was empowered by Yahweh's Spirit, so Jesus was empowered by the Spirit of God.*
- *The work that Samson did as Judge, he did alone. Jesus accomplished His work alone.*
- *The last act Samson did as Judge was to sacrifice his life to destroy the enemy. Jesus sacrificed His life to destroy him who had the power of death, the devil. Samson, as he stretched out to push the pillars apart, prefigured the cross.*

What can we learn from the Samson narrative that will give us hope?

As Samson was set apart prior to his birth, so are we. According to Paul in Ephesians 1, the saints of God have been chosen in Christ before the foundation of the World. Thus, prior to our births, we were known and called by God to serve him.

The Spirit that "came mightily upon" Samson is the same Spirit who indwells us. The Spirit did not indwell Samson which is why the Spirit left Samson. Samson did his mighty deeds in the strength of the Spirit.

As Samson called upon Yahweh in his deep hour of distress, we too can call upon God in our distress. But we have a greater privilege / duty. We are to be unceasingly in communication with God. This is possible for the indwelling Spirit enables us to call God Father. Samson did not know Yahweh as father.

Yahweh's Spirit came upon Samson and enabled Samson to do various feats of strength even though Samson broke the Nazarite vow. Yet, Samson held onto the most visible aspect of the vow and therefore he was used of Yahweh to confront Covenantal obligation as well as Covenantal abrogation.

The whole of the Samson and woman of Timnah narrative is an example of the truth revealed in Deuteronomy 29:29, "The secret things belong to the LORD our God, but those things which are revealed belong to us and to our children forever, that we may do all the words of this law." This side of the resurrected and ascended Jesus, we may confidently know that everything in our lives is being used of God to conform us to His son. Samson's parents did not have that sure word.

> *As a priest, a piece of mere church furniture at best.*
> -William Cowper, Triocinium line 425

Eli – The Priest

The first we encounter Eli, "the priest," he is sitting on the seat by the doorpost of the Temple. His two sons, Hophni and Phineas were performing the priestly duties. There is no record of Eli performing the tasks of the Judges as outlined in Judges 2:18-19. It is only in Eli's death notice that we are told he judged Israel forty years. The corruption of the leadership in Israel is graphically manifested in Eli and his sons. Eli has little influence in Israel or with his sons. His sons were corrupt not knowing Yahweh. The book of Judges closed with "everyone did what was right in their own eyes." Hophni and Phineas were priests who did whatever they deemed right using their position as priests to their own advantage.[295] Yet it is Eli that Yahweh holds responsible for his sons' behavior.[296]

Eli's death notice is given as Eli hears the news that his sons were killed and the Ark of God was taken. Following their defeat at the hand of the Philistines, the elders of Israel wondered why Yahweh had defeated them. They decided to bring the Ark of the Covenant from Shiloh to the battle scene. The thinking was that the presence of the Ark would deliver them from the power of their enemies. When the Ark arrived in camp, Israel expected victory and the Philistines were full of fear and in trepidation. The Philistines rallied themselves with the exhortation to be men and fight. Israel was defeated, Hophni and Phineas killed, and the Ark of the Covenant taken. The capture of the Ark is the nadir of the period of the Judges. 1 Samuel 6 and 7 record Yahweh's war against the Philistines and the resolution of that war. The Ark was eventually returned to Kiriath-jearim, but did not return to its proper place until the time of David.

Eli died at age ninety eight years old. If he retired at age fifty,[297] Eli had forty-eight years of no work but he was available to assist. If Samuel began his service at age thirty, then Eli could have been in his sixties as he sat by the doorpost of the Temple in 1 Samuel 1:9. Eli was then given the task of mentoring Samuel at least twenty years. This is what is called a "second chance." Eli as judge, father, and priest, based on his sons' behavior and the conditions that lead to the taking of the Ark, was an abysmal failure. But Eli's Covenant God gave Eli an opportunity for "redemption."

Eli's supposition that Hannah was drinking would be consistent with the culture of Israel at the time. When Hannah explained that she was pouring out her soul to Yahweh, Eli blessed her. Samuel being brought to Eli after being weaned became the charge of Eli. Immediately following the statement that Samuel ministered to Yahweh before Eli the priest, we are told that Eli's sons were corrupt and did not know Yahweh. This juxtaposition accentuates the "second chance" opportunity Yahweh gives Eli.

Eli was used of Yahweh to bless Hannah and Elkanah, and to teach Samuel to identify Yahweh's voice. As priest, Eli was to speak on behalf of men to God. Eli's sphere of influence seemed to be limited to Elkanah's family and specifically Samuel. Yet through mentoring Samuel, Eli influenced the future of Israel. Yahweh cursed the house of Eli yet the man was used to mentor the one who would be the last judge and first prophet in the new theocratic era.[298]

Twice Eli is identified as "the priest." As priest he is a forerunner of Jesus. His foreshadowing of Jesus as priest is not complete for Jesus is our High Priest. His activity in the life of Elkanah's family and in Samuel foreshadow Jesus as Eli blesses and leads Samuel in his service to Yahweh. Eli also foreshadows Jesus as his concern is not for his sons but the Ark of God.[299] This concern reveals that Eli, despite his failures, understood what was truly important and his heart was committed to Yahweh. Eli is deeply flawed, but very dimly speaks of Jesus.

Eli may dimly testify of Jesus, but Eli teaches us that our God always has something for His people to do. As long as we have breath, we have the privilege of serving our God. As Yahweh allowed for "retirement" at age fifty, He also expected those "retired" to assist. What better way to assist than to mentor the young? Eli may have been a less than stellar father for his sons, but Yahweh placed him in the position to mentor Samuel. Think of the years of reflection Eli had prior to

> **Eli may dimly testify of Jesus, but Eli teaches us that our God always has something for His people to do. As long as we have breath, we have the privilege of serving our God.**

receiving Samuel as a disciple. Is not Eli a wonderful example of someone who, after a life of learning, became an example of the exhortation for older men to be sober, reverent, temperate, sound in faith, in love, and in patience?[300] The Scriptures do not tell us how Eli failed. We only see the results of his failure. But we do see how Eli fulfilled his calling as Samuel's mentor. Rejoice and be glad for the Lord is always molding us and shaping us to be fruitful workers in His Kingdom.

A God-intoxicated man.
-Friedrich von Hardenberg remarking about Spinoza.

Samuel – Judge, Priest, and Prophet

Samuel is the only Judge whose activity overlaps the activity of another Judge. Samuel filled the role of prophet before he became Judge. As a young prophet, he brought the word of Yahweh to Eli,[301] and gained a reputation in Israel as a prophet of Yahweh.[302] After King Saul is established, Samuel continues as prophet and is recognized as the first prophet in the new theocratic order.[303] This prophetic function is demonstrated by confronting Saul with the word of Yahweh,[304] and anointing David king.[305]

Following the death of Eli, Samuel becomes the last Judge. In the capacity of Judge, Samuel induced the people to turn to Yahweh, remove idols, and engage the Philistines in combat again.[306] As in other battles during the judge era, Yahweh intervened bringing about a great victory for His people.[307] Samuel as priest offered a sacrifice and prayed to Yahweh.[308] Yahweh honored Samuel's intercession and defeated the

Philistines. This is analogous to the battle fought by Israel under Moses when Israel won because Moses held his hands up.[309] Following the victory over the Philistines, Samuel entered into a judgeship which was itinerant in nature.[310] He was involved in adjudicating cases and leading the people in worship.

As the last judge, Samuel clarified all that the Judges were to be. When Samuel transferred his administrative duties to the king, he maintained his responsibilities to pray for the Sons of Israel and to instruct them.[311]

By retaining the responsibility to instruct, Samuel retains the role of prophet. By retaining the responsibility to pray, Samuel retains the role of priest.

By retaining the responsibility to instruct, Samuel retains the role of prophet. By retaining the responsibility to pray, Samuel retains the role of priest. Thus the role Samuel "gave up" was the role of king. Therefore all the Judges fulfilled the roles of prophet, priest, and king. A prophet speaks on behalf of God to men. A priest speaks on behalf of men to God. A king was to administer the law of God and be subject to that same law. Ultimately a rejection of the one whom Yahweh raised up to be Judge was a rejection of Yahweh.[312]

As Prophet, Priest, and King, Samuel testifies of Jesus. Jesus, the Word,[313] speaks to men of God. Jesus is the ultimate Word from God to men.[314]

As a child of God redeemed by the blood of Jesus and robed in His righteousness, you are a prophet, priest, and king.

As priest, Jesus is a priest forever, is a mediator of a greater covenant, and offers the only sacrifice that transforms men and provides a complete remedy for sin.[315] Furthermore, Jesus our High Priest, intercedes for us.[316] Jesus is King for all authority in heaven and earth is vested in Him and He reigns forever.[317]

Let us, as pilgrims and sojourners on Earth and citizens of heaven, exercise our privileges as prophets, priests, and kings.

Ask yourself...

- *Do I now realize that prior to my birth I was called by God to serve Him?*

- *What feats of strength would God have me do in the power of His Spirit?*
- *Do I now see that the Spirit that "came mightily upon" Samson is the same Spirit who indwells me?*
- *Do I call upon God in my distress expecting Him to answer me?*
- *Am I confident that everything in my life is being used of God to conform me to His son?*

Here are some action steps you can start with today.

- God always has something for His people to do. As long as we have breath, we have the privilege of serving our God. Seek God for what it is He has for you to do.
- Rejoice and be glad for the Lord is always molding and shaping us to be fruitful workers in His Kingdom. Go about whatever God has given you to do today full of joy and thanksgiving.
- As a child of God redeemed by the blood of Jesus and robed in His righteousness, you are a prophet, priest, and king.

As prophet you are to let no corrupt word proceed out of your mouth, but what is good for necessary edification, that it may impart grace to the hearers, rebuke those who are sinning, and instruct those weak in the faith. Read Ephesians 4:29; 1 Timothy 5:20; Galatians 2:11-21; and Romans 14.

As a priest you are to offer up:
- your body as a living sacrifice – read Romans 12:1-2.
- the sacrifice of praise–read Psalm 54:6 and Hebrews 13:15.
- the sacrifice of our treasure – read Philippians 4:10-20.
- the incense of prayer–read Revelation 5:8 and Exodus 30:1-10, 34-38.

Your prayers are sweet incense before the Lord. You are to pray without ceasing, and for all men. Your prayers are to be fervent. An example of one who prayed fervently is Epaphrus who wrestled in prayer. Read Colossians 4:12. Another example of strenuous prayer is Jacob by the ford of Jabbok. Read Genesis 32:22-31.

As a king you are to administer the law of Christ or the Royal Law. Read Galatians 6:2 and James 2:8.

You are to judge angels therefore you are not to go to the world for adjudication, but to resolve things within the Body of Christ. If not resolved, you ought to be willing to be cheated and commit all to God. Read 1 Corinthians 6:1-11 and Romans 12:12-21.

Chapter 10

Israel's Apostasy Necessitated Judges

> *Therefore whoever hears these sayings of Mine, and does them, I will liken him to a wise man who built his house on the rock: and the rain descended, the floods came, and the winds blew and beat on that house; and it did not fall, for it was founded on the rock.*
>
> *But everyone who hears these sayings of Mine, and does not do them will be like a foolish man who built his house on the sand: and the rain descended, the floods came, and the winds blew and beat on that house; and it fell. And great was its fall. (Matthew 7:24-27)*

The writer of the Book of Judges in chapters 3-16 tells us of those whom Yahweh raised up to deliver the Sons of Israel. Throughout the narrative, Yahweh demonstrates His faithfulness to the Covenant made at Sinai. The Sinaitic Covenant was the "legal" document that bound Yahweh to Israel, defining Israel as a nation and acknowledging that Yahweh was Israel's King. This relationship of Yahweh to Israel was rooted in the Covenant Yahweh made with Abraham, Isaac, and Jacob. Yahweh had given the Sons of Israel a vocation: "You shall be a special treasure to Me above all people; for all the earth is Mine. And you shall be to Me a kingdom of priests and a holy nation." The vocation given to the Sons of Israel was predicated on Exodus 19:6 which says, "Now therefore, if you will indeed obey My voice and keep My covenant, then you shall be a special treasure to Me above all people." The Sons of Israel ratified the Covenant saying, "All that Yahweh has spoken we will do." Following the giving of the Decalogue, the people went to Moses saying, "You speak with us, and we will hear; but let not God speak with us, lest we die." They were never to fulfill their vocation. The vocation is fulfilled in Christ and the new covenant.[318]

The chief office within the Covenantal community was the office of priest.[319] The priest was to be an intermediary between Yahweh and man. Moses was the first Priest in

> **The chief office within the Covenantal community was the office of priest.**

the Covenantal community. It was Moses who was to consecrate Aaron and his sons.[320] It was Moses who interceded for the people and was prepared to offer himself for the people.[321] Moses and Aaron were of the tribe of Levi.

Each tribe was given an inheritance in the Promised Land. The Levites inheritance was to be the offering by fire to Yahweh.[322] The Levites were to be scattered throughout Israel in forty-eight cities apportioned according to the size of each tribe.[323] These cities were to be teaching centers and places of maintaining the law in Israel, six of which were cities of refuge. But as the last five chapters of Judges and the narrative of Eli and his sons demonstrate, the priests failed. Hence the need for prophets who called the people back to the Law. They showed God's power and mercy especially to the righteous remnant despite the general wickedness to the people as a whole. Failure of the priesthood and of the Levites continuing instruction and discipline were why judges were necessary.

The final five chapters of Judges, consisting of two narratives, are an epilogue graphically describing the state of anarchy that existed in the absence of knowledge of the Law and

> **Israel rejected the Kingship of Yahweh and pursued life in the manner that suited them.**

obedience to it. Wandering Levites are at the center of both stories. They were not where they should be nor doing what they should be doing. Concerned for their own physical needs and desires, they neglected their Covenantal duties.

The Sons of Israel were to be the vassal to the Covenant King, Yahweh. But the phrase, "there was no king in Israel," appears four times in chapters 17-21: after Micah consecrated his sons, just prior to the narrative regarding the tribe Dan's migration, prior to the narrative regarding the Levite and the tribe of Benjamin, and the last sentence in the Book of Judges. Thus, Israel rejected the Kingship of Yahweh and pursued life in the manner that suited them. Eventually they asked for a king like all the other nations. With that request they made clear their rejection of Yahweh as King.[324] Having rejected the King, the representatives of the King became part of the problem or possibly the root of the problem.

According to the terms of the Covenant ratified at Sinai, Israel's rejection of Yahweh as King subjected Israel to discipline. The terms of the Covenant included blessing for obedience and curses for disobedience. The blessings that were to be enjoyed by the Sons of Israel, if they fulfilled their vow are recorded in Deuteronomy 28:1-14. The curses resulting from disobedience are recorded in Deuteronomy 28:15-68. Moses summarizes the blessings and curses at the end of the Covenant Renewal in Moab.

> *See, I have set before you today life and good, death and evil, in that I command you today to love Yahweh your God, to walk in His ways, and to keep His commandments, His statutes, and His judgments, that you may live and multiply; and Yahweh your God will bless you in the land which you go to possess. But if your heart turns away so that you do not hear, and are drawn away, and worship other gods and serve them, I announce to you today that you shall surely perish; you shall not prolong your days in the land which you cross over the Jordan to go in and possess. I call heaven and earth as witnesses today against you, that I have set before you life and death, blessing and cursing; therefore choose life, that both you and your descendants may live; that you may love Yahweh your God, that you may obey His voice, and that you may cling to Him, for He is your life and the length of your days; and that you may dwell in the land which Yahweh swore to your fathers, to Abraham, Isaac, and Jacob, to give them. (Deuteronomy 30:15-20).*

The Deliverers were raised up to draw the Sons of Israel back to their Covenant King.[325] During the life of the judges, God provided physical deliverance from punishment for idolatry when the people cried out to

Him, a priestly activity. But the general spiritual state was anarchy and the lives of the judges themselves were often severe mixtures of good and evil.

It is probable that the events in Judges 17 and 18 are connected to Judges 1:34 which states that the Amorites would not let the Danites into the valley. Thus it is probable

If the foundations are destroyed, What can the righteous do? (**Psalm 11:3**)

that the events of Judges 17 and 18 occur prior to Othniel or during the forty years of rest under Othniel. These two chapters reveal perversion of the Sinaitic Covenant and how Yahweh, the Lord of all the Earth, was made like the gods of the other nations. Chapters 19-21 occur during the time Phinehas, the grandson of Aaron, served as Priest.[326]

The foundation of the Nation of Israel was its Covenant with Yahweh ratified at Sinai. The last five chapters of Judges graphically demonstrate that the foundation was destroyed within two generations of Aaron, the high priest at Sinai. As we meditate on the last five chapters consider the Psalmist's question, "If the foundations are destroyed, what can the righteous do?"

Religious Perversion Results in Sin and Delusion

> *A man and a lion were discussing the relative strength of men and lions in general. The man contended that he and his fellows were stronger than lions by reason of their greater intelligence. "Come now with me," he cried, "and I will prove that I am right." So he took him into the public gardens and showed him a statue of Hercules overcoming the lion and tearing his mouth in two. "That is all very well," said the lion, "but proves nothing, for it was a man who made the statue." We can easily represent things as we wish them to be. -Aesop's Fables, "The Lion and the Statue"*

Micah, an Ephraimite, stole money from his mother. She, upon discovering the theft, curses the thief. Hearing his mother curse the thief, Micah returns the money to her. In response his mother blesses him in the name of Yahweh. Micah was a novice in sin, for his mother's imprecation upon the thief caused him to return the money. Micah feared the curse.

He did not fear Yahweh for he stole breaking the eighth commandment. His mother, demonstrating her mistaken understanding of Yahweh, blesses her son and states that she had dedicated the whole sum to Yahweh.

Micah and his mother proceed to use some of the money in fashioning a graven image thus breaking the second commandment. The remaining money apparently was used to procure the various articles and garments to complete the shrine. The shrine included an ephod which was a garment to be worn by the high priest.[327] Micah, having the necessary furniture and garments, lacked a priest. Therefore, Micah consecrates one of his sons as priest.[328] Micah had taken it upon himself to disregard the requirements for worshiping Yahweh and devised his own ways which were a perversion of the requirements given by Yahweh.

Micah had taken it upon himself to disregard the requirements for worshiping Yahweh and devised his own ways which were a perversion of the requirements given by Yahweh.

What was the explanation for such gross perversions? The writer tells us, "...there was no king in Israel; everyone did what was right in his own eyes." There was no authority to convince Micah of his sin in making an image and shrine. There was no one to inflict a consequence upon such flagrant disregard for the Sinaitic Covenant. Ultimately, there was the rejection of the Covenant King and disregard of the blessings and curses of the Sinaitic Covenant. Thus every man became his own adjudicator and "blessed" his own life. Hence we have: the cursing then blessing from Micah's mother over money; devotion to making an idol, no godly discipline of her child, only greed and outward show.

Micah's perversion is not isolated. The narrative continues to tell us of a Levite who sojourned in Bethlehem in Judah and got the "wanderlust." Bethlehem was not a Levitical city and therefore not an appropriate place for a Levite to live. He left Bethlehem with no particular destination in mind and came to the house of Micah. Micah invited the Levite to be a father and a priest in Micah's household. The Levite had no intention of tarrying, but Micah's invitation enticed him and he stayed. Micah's invitation provided the Levite with a livelihood in his "profession." Thus Micah's shrine was complete for he had a Levite, one designated by the Sinaitic Covenant to be priest. Micah took this provision as a sign that Yahweh would bless him.

Having no king in Israel did not only affect individuals, it also affected the tribe of Dan. Dan had been given an inheritance bordered by the Mediterranean Sea.[329] But the children of Dan had trouble enjoying their inheritance,[330] so they went beyond what had been given them.[331] The children of Dan sent five men to scout out the land for further settlement. While on their mission they came to the house of Micah and recognized the voice of the Levite. After inquiring about why he was there and what he was doing, they asked the Levite to inquire of God to determine if they would be successful. The priest said that they should go in peace and that Yahweh would be with them.

The men who were sent to scout out the land came upon the people of Laish who were living peaceably and at ease in their rich fertile valley. They had no thought that they were in danger. The people of Laish lived after the manner of the Sidonians whose habitual security was a consequence of their location by the sea and their pursuit of commerce. The Sidonians were little concerned with the wars going on around them because they were too busy becoming rich. Thus the people of Laish were at peace also. The scouts returned to their home with the report that "god has given" this rich fertile land in our hands for the people are secure, thus not ready to defend. Six hundred men of war departed for Laish.

On their way to Laish, the six hundred camped in Judah and passed into the mountains of Ephraim. The five scouts remembered the shrine they had seen in Micah's house. The group turned aside, showed up at Micah's house, bought the priest, and stole the shrine. The Danites put their children and goods in front of them as they left Micah's house. The men in the neighborhood, who probably worshiped at Micah's shrine, followed, caught up to the Danites, and called out to them. The Danites turned and asked, "What ails you." Micah's problem was his loss of God, shrine, priest, and all that he had. The Danites responded with an admonishment and threat. Micah succumbed and returned home.

The children of Dan continued on their way with the loot from Micah's house. Arriving at Laish they struck the peaceful citizens with the sword and burned the city. There was no one for the citizens to call upon for help for their natural allies, the Sidonians, were far away. Thus a portion of the Tribe of Dan entered the fertile Valley, rebuilt the city calling it Dan, and settled down. In settling down they established a place of worship with the stolen articles from Micah. They also set the Levite,

Jonathan the son of Gershom, as priest establishing his family as their priestly line. The Danites prove the anti-Platonic "rule of the stronger." This resulted in a "new exodus" to live in isolation from priest/tabernacle and do one's own thing.

The writer of Judges is careful to point out that the place of worship for the Sons of Israel remained in Shiloh as it was throughout the whole of the Judge Era.[332] It would seem that the woeful tale of Micah, his priest, and the Danites would not provide us with hope nor testify of Jesus. The tale moves from sin to sin culminating in establishing an "anti – Shiloh" that plagued the Sons of Israel until Israel, the Northern Kingdom, was carried into captivity.[333] The focus of the tale is the establishment of an alternative place of worship, first for an individual then for a tribe. The establishment of the alternative place of worship is attributed to there being no king in Israel. According to Judges 17:6, the standard or law that men used to adjudicate their behavior was their personal evaluation. Yet throughout the sordid tale, the Sinaitic Covenant casts a long shadow that gets dimmer as the tale progresses.

Micah, his mother, and the Levite had some idea of Yahweh but their understanding was perverted. In their perversion, they understood that the Covenant God: was the one by whom people were blessed, was worthy of worship, would prosper obedience, and granted guidance to those He approved. Though they used the Covenant God's name, they knew not the Covenant God. Their skewed concept of Yahweh foreshadowed the skewed concept of the Messiah held by the Jews in the Gospels. The Jews of the Gospels expected a Messiah who would restore the fortunes of Israel as they were in the days of David and Solomon. But the Messiah, as foretold and revealed, is the King of kings who has all authority in Heaven and Earth. His Kingdom is not of this world nor is it temporal. The Jews were myopic and proud in their ignorance as were Micah and his mother. Micah, his mother, and the Levite knew the name of Yahweh and made Him who is the creator of Heaven and Earth to be a local god fashioned by the hand of man. Thus they accepted Yahweh on their terms and not on Yahweh's terms, exchanging the Creator for the creature. Similarly, the Jews of the Gospels crucified the Lord of Glory because they refused to accept Jesus on Jesus' terms.

The Sons of Dan did not acknowledge Yahweh, but did acknowledge divinity. Their perversion had plumbed to the depth of denying a Covenant

God. The god they had in mind was a god to call upon when their own strength and guile were found lacking. Yet they retained some understanding for the need of a priest and place of worship. Once again within wrongheaded thinking we see a foreshadowing of Jesus. The need for a priest and a sacred place was the tacit confession that a man cannot approach the Divine without a mediator. Thus their tacit confession foreshadowed the mediatory role of Jesus, the one mediator between God and man.

What do we learn from Micah, his mother, the Levite, and the Sons of Dan? Consider the patience of God. In 1 Corinthians 13:4-8a, love is defined by fifteen elements. The very first element is patience. This sordid tale would never have reached completion if Yahweh had dealt with Micah and his mother as He had dealt with the Covenant breakers at Mount Sinai.[334] Micah and his mother did no more or less than the Covenant breakers at Mount Sinai but they lived. So too, the Levite and the Sons of Dan benefited from the patience of Yahweh. Paul tells us that God's patience is intended to bring us to repentance.[335] Peter tells us to think of God's patience as an opportunity to be saved.[336] Do you think Micah, his mother or someone in the neighborhood repented when their idol and shrine proved to be nothing at all?

> **Consider the patience of God and remember that His patience is an opportunity to be saved.**

Let us consider the patience of Yahweh with respect to the chronology of Judges 17 and 18. These events took place early in the Judge Era. The cycle of rebellion, oppression, repentance, deliverance, and rebellion that characterizes Judges 3-16 was in its early stages. Yet the "anti-Shiloh" in Dan was established and was a snare for the Sons of Israel during the whole of the Judge Era and for many more years. Consider the patience of God and remember that His patience is an opportunity to be saved.

Ask Yourself...

- *What is the foundation of my life? Am I secure enough not to be swayed by peer pressure, eloquent words or circumstances that cause consternation and doubt?*
- *What is the only foundation that is unshakable even though all else is destroyed?*

- *What is the spiritual state of: my soul, my church, and my family?*
- *How did Micah, his mother, the Levite, and tribe of Dan break the third commandment: "You shall not take the name of the Lord your God in vain"?*
- *How can I guard against doing as they did?*

Here are some action steps you can start with today.

- How does God want to be worshiped? Read John 4:19-24. Begin to worship as this instructs.
- How has God demonstrated His patience with you?
- What have you done as a result of God's patience?
- What more do you need to do to truly worship God as you now know He requires?
- Consider the patience of God and remember that His patience is an opportunity to be saved.

Chapter 11

WANDERING LEVITE AND THE "NEW SODOM"

Other kids games are all such a bore!
They've gotta have rules and they gotta keep score!
Calvinball is better by far!
It's never the same! It's always bizarre!
You don't need a team or a referee!
You know that it's great, cause it's named after me!
If you wanna...
"Calvin and Hobbes" Comic Strip, 11 September 1995
by Bill Watterson

The last three chapters of Judges is a narrative that begins with, "And it came to pass in those days, when there was no king in Israel," and ends with, "In those days there was no king in Israel; everyone did what was right in his own eyes." There being no king in Israel, any possible semblance of Covenantal authority would be with the Levites. Any proper exercise of Covenantal worship would be administered by the Levites at Shiloh. But a Levite in the hill country of Ephraim was a bit like a "fish out of water." There would be no "proper work" for the Levite in the hill country, but he still would have an "air" of authority. The young Levite who was hired by Micah is an example of vagrant or out of work Levites. When he took Micah's offer it may have been a case of any job being better than none. When offered a more lucrative and influential position by the Sons

Everyone did what was right in his own eyes.

of Dan, he is an example of one who prostitutes himself, committing the sin of Balaam.[337] In chapter nineteen there is a Levite living in the hill country of Ephraim, another place not designated for the Levites.

We are not told the occupation of the Levite in chapter nineteen, but we are told that he took a concubine from Bethlehem. Concubines are "second class" wives. Three notable concubines are Hagar, Abraham's concubine, and Bilhah and Zilpah, who were the concubines of Jacob. Playing the harlot, the concubine returned to her father's house in Bethlehem, and stayed four months. The Levite, instead of having his concubine burned,[338] went to her father's house to seek her to be reconciled. His intention was to speak tenderly to her and take her back to his home. Having a concubine behave as a harlot ought to have been a great embarrassment to one who was to be serving in the "House of Yahweh." In spite of what ought to have been, the Levite pursued his concubine to woo her back to his home. In this the Levite is a forerunner of Hosea and foreshadows Jesus. The prophet Hosea is the Old Testament character who comes closest to the New Testament revelation of God's love. The heart of Hosea's message revolves around the word *chesed* which is a covenant word implying covenant loyalty. Applied to Yahweh it means mercy and loving kindness: loyal love and covenanted mercies. The Levite in pursuing his unfaithful concubine manifests loyal love and mercy.

The Levite in pursuing his unfaithful concubine manifests loyal love and mercy.

A journey of love and mercy changes character as the concubine's father "wines and dines" the Levite for four and a half days. It can be concluded that there was nothing in the Mountains of Ephraim that demanded the Levite's attention for he frittered away his time in Bethlehem. Being welcomed by his father-in-law, the Levite stayed three days eating and drinking. After three days the Levite attempted to leave in the early morning, but he was detained by more food and drink. On the fifth day, he attempted to leave in the early morning, but was detained again by food until the afternoon.

The distance from Bethlehem to his home was probably between fifteen and thirty-five miles. A "Day's Journey" would be about seven or eight hours or approximately twenty-five to thirty miles. According to what the Levite told the old man in Gibeah, their destination was apparently Shiloh which was about twenty-five to thirty miles from Bethlehem. If the Levite had left at dawn it is highly probable that he would be in Shiloh by dusk, but he delayed. Consequently the Levite, his concubine, and his servant had to spend one night on the road.

They had left Bethlehem so late in the day that the Levite's servant suggested they stop for the night in Jebus (Jerusalem) which was a distance of five to seven miles or about two hours. But the Levite determined to "push on" because he did not want to lodge with "foreigners," but with the children of Israel. The small group pushed on for another hour or so. Arriving in Gibeah of Benjamin, they prepared to spend the night in the city square since, contrary to customary practices of hospitality, no one offered them lodging.

A sojourner in Gibeah who had been working in the field, presumably all day, welcomed the Levite and his entourage into his home. The old man opened his home and provided all necessities for man and beast even though the Levite had enough of his own provisions. As they were delighting in one another's company, both being from the Mountains of Ephraim, they were interrupted by men of the city who wished to abuse the Levite.

Any tenderness the Levite had for his concubine evaporated in Gibeah because, to save his own neck, he gave her to the men of Gibeah to use as they wished. Rather than trust Yahweh, who he was to serve and represent, he placated the rabble by tossing his concubine to them. As she was being abused, he was at rest. Rising to go, he admonished her to rise and get going. His insensitivity to his concubine's plight became outrage as he roused the tribes of Israel to administer justice (or was it revenge) upon the men of Gibeah by sending dismembered portions of his concubine's body throughout Israel.

Demonstrating the "authority" held by the Levites, the Sons of Israel gathered to hear the Levite's story. Following the telling of the tale, the Levite asked for their collective counsel. Having heard the squalid tale, they determined that the guilty should be punished. Emissaries were sent to the Tribe of Benjamin asking the Benjamites to give up those who were guilty. Refusing to comply with the request, the Benjamites aligned themselves with their guilty brethren. As a result of the Benjamites aligning with their guilty brethren, the Sons of Israel engaged in three battles with the Tribe of Benjamin nearly destroying that tribe.

Before each of the battles the Sons of Israel inquired of Yahweh. The first inquiry was to find out who should lead the battle. Yahweh said that Judah should be first. After the defeat of the first battle, a period of weeping preceded their inquiry concerning going against Benjamin again. Benjamin defeated the Sons of Israel a second time. A day of weeping and fasting followed by burnt offerings and peace offerings preceded the third inquiry of Yahweh. Also noted were the presence of the Ark of the Covenant and the High Priest. Yahweh responded to the third inquiry with the assurance of victory. The third battle resulted in the decimation of the Tribe of Benjamin.

Originally the guilty of Gibeah were to pay the price required by the Sons of Israel for the abasement and death of the Levite's concubine. As events fell out, the price of the sin of Gibeah was thousands dead of the Sons of Israel and the near destruction of the Tribe of Benjamin. A rash vow by the Sons of Israel not to give their daughters as wives to the Benjamites resulted in more death and scheming so that the genocide of Benjamin would not result in a tribe of Israel being lost. Having "saved" Benjamin from extinction, all returned to their inheritance pursuing their own agendas.

Judges 19-21 is a narrative of a society of prosperity without law, priest or gospel.[339] A multitude of events occur as a result of the ignorance of Yahweh's law or rebellion against that law. Beginning with a Levite in the wrong place doing something other than his proper vocation, the narrative's focus is on the rejection of Yahweh as King and the consequences of that rejection. But within the narrative there are glimpses of Jesus.

Early the Levite demonstrates love and forgiveness as he pursues his concubine to woo her in spite of her harlotry. Throughout the Old Testament harlotry is a picture of Israel's faithlessness as she pursues foreign gods. Yet, Yahweh continues to send His prophets calling His people back to their Covenant responsibilities and privileges. But the Levite loses focus in frivolity and then becomes indifferent when personally threatened. Thus the Levite fails to demonstrate a love that "never fails". As Jesus implied, there are degrees of love; "Greater love has no one than this, than to lay down one's life for his friends." The Levite loved his concubine enough to pursue her and win her back, but not enough to keep her from the abuse of the rabble. He was not willing to give his life for the concubine. His limited love, as crippled as it is, points to the one who loves His people with an everlasting love and gave His life that they may live.

As men are convicted of sin they turn to the priest for guidance and instruction. But as the narrative unfolds, not all sin is addressed. The Levite's sin of idleness[340] was the cause of the necessity to spend the night in Gibeah, the Israelite Sodom, a city of great sin. But the tribes of Israel were not roused against the city until the Levite sent the dismembered concubine throughout Israel. Until then the attitude was "live and let live." Having been roused by the Levite, they gathered to punish the guilty. Conviction of sin was the result of the horrific crime, not as a result of the sin. How often do we ignore sin until it impinges upon our life?

> *In Germany, they came first for the Communists, and I didn't speak up because I wasn't Communist. Then they came for the trade unionists, and I didn't speak up because I wasn't a trade unionist. Then they came for the Jews, and I didn't speak up because I wasn't a Jew. And then, they came for "me," Christians, and by that time there was no one left to speak up.* –Pastor Marin Niemoeller (1891-1984)

Initially only the men of Gibeah were to be punished. Since the Gibeahites were members of the Tribe of Benjamin, Benjamin was asked to "give up" the guilty. But rather than punish the guilty, the Benjamites aligned themselves with the guilty becoming accomplices. How often do we become accomplices of sin as a result of our unwillingness to confront, reprove, rebuke, and possibly disassociate? This initial attempt to address the sin of Gibeah was the fruit of the Levite's diatribe and the mass response to it. Yahweh was not consulted. Was the Levite a sufficient authority for the Sons of Israel?

Yahweh was consulted after the Tribe of Benjamin aligned themselves with the guilty. Yahweh was consulted three times. The first two attempts to punish the guilty resulted in failure and death. The third attempt to address the guilty was successful, but at the price of near total destruction of the Tribe of Benjamin. Each consultation with Yahweh is instructive. The first consultation was to inquire of Yahweh concerning leadership. Judah was designated as the leader of the Tribes. The second consultation was preceded by weeping. They had already made up their mind and were looking for Divine approbation. Much the same way people look for "proof texts" in the Scripture to defend their sinful behavior. Both of these consultations resulted in defeat. The third consultation was preceded by weeping, fasting, burnt offerings, and peace offerings. Can we conclude that the weeping prior to the second consultation was remorse?[341] Can we then conclude that the weeping, fasting, and offerings prior to the third consultation involved repentance?[342]

This third consultation is most instructive. It is here that the Ark of the Covenant is mentioned in conjunction with the High Priest and the burnt offerings and peace offerings. It is the only reference to the Ark and the High Priest in the Book of Judges.

The Ark, the High Priest, the burnt offering, and the peace offering speak of Jesus.

According to the Sinaitic Covenant, Yahweh was to be approached in a specific manner. Burnt offerings and peace offerings were necessary to approach Yahweh as He had specified. The Ark was the symbol of Yahweh's presence and was kept in the Holy of Holies. The High Priest was the only priest permitted inside the Holy of Holies, and that but once a year with blood. Yahweh responds to the third inquiry with the assurance that the Benjamites would be delivered to the Sons of Israel. The first two inquiries resulted in discipline that eventually drove the Sons of Israel back to Yahweh on Yahweh's terms.

It is the third inquiry that gives us the testimony regarding Jesus. The Ark, the High Priest, the burnt offering, and the peace offering speak of Jesus. The Ark was the symbol of the presence of God among His people. Jesus, in His person, is Immanuel, God with us. His presence is ever with His saints as He said to His disciples, "I am with you always, even to the end of the age." Jesus is our High Priest who ever

That the Creator of Heaven and Earth will hear the cry of the penitent is a great hope.

intercedes for us.[343] All the sacrifices of the Old Testament foreshadow the sacrifice of Jesus which cleanses from all sin.[344] Jesus is our peace.[345] Through Jesus we have peace with God[346] and are able to enjoy the peace of God.[347]

As we meditate on the last three chapters of Judges, is it possible to derive any hope? Consider the depth of sin exposed in these three chapters. The Covenant People, having rejected their King, became fragmented and each faction became a law to themselves; becoming so sinful that the consequences of sin impinged upon others' lives and had to be addressed. The sin being addressed was compounded as those who sought redress consulted not their king but themselves. After failure, they addressed their King on His terms and the remedy to the evil was found. Sin compounding sin made the price of the remedy very high. So how is hope derived from this? We are to address God on His terms. If we address Him on His terms, He will hear us. That the Creator of Heaven and Earth will hear the cry of the penitent is a great hope.

When we meditate on the main characters of the last three chapters, we catch glimpses of the character of Yahweh. The Levite's love, shallow as it was, still gives us hope that we, by God's grace, may learn to love even our enemies. In spite of the rejection of the Covenant King, Yahweh used His designated representatives, the Levite and High Priest to call His people to Himself, however briefly. Therefore, we who are called, sent, and equipped may have hope that the One who called, sent, and equipped us will use us for His glory and the church's edification.

> **The greatest hope given by these three chapters is we are not without a King.**

The greatest hope given by these three chapters is that we are not without a King. Our King indwells us by His Spirit who gifts us to do the will of our Redeemer and King. As members of the Body of Christ we are never in a position "to do that which is right in our own eyes." Our hearts of stone have been made flesh and we, as we grow in the grace and knowledge of Jesus, will delight to obey our King.

Ask Yourself...

- *What are three things that have changed in my life as a result of becoming a member of the Kingdom of God and submitting to our King, Jesus?*
- *How is the Kingship of Jesus manifested in my congregation? How does my congregation convey to the World that the Kingdom of God has come and is represented by my church?*
- *Jesus is the King of kings who has given us the task of making disciples (Matthew 28:18-20). What have I done in the past year to advance His kingdom?*

- *How do I, as a citizen of Heaven, influence my world ? Am I the Salt and Light I am designed to be?*

Here are some action steps you can start with today.

Discover the terms whereby we are to address God using the scriptures listed below.

- Psalm 66:18 says if I have _____ _____
  God will not hear me.
- 1 Peter 3:7 says my prayers are hindered if _____
- Philippians 4:6 says all prayer must be accompanied by _____
  _____

- John 14:13, 14; 15:16; 16:23-26 says I am to approach the throne of grace with _____
  _____

Chapter 12

ONE MORE NARRATIVE

For wherever you go, I will go; and wherever you lodge I will lodge; your people shall be my people, and your God, my God. Where you die, I will die, and there will I be buried. Yahweh do so to me, and more also, if anything but death parts you and me. (Ruth 1:16-17)

The cycle of rebellion, oppression, repentance, deliverance, and rebellion that characterizes Judges is a backdrop that magnifies the faithfulness of Yahweh and graphically demonstrates the Psalmist's assertion that Yahweh, the shepherd, accompanies His people "through the valley of the shadow of death." One more narrative from the Judge Era draws us to wonder as the Providence of Yahweh works in the darkness to provide for the fulfillment of Yahweh's Covenant with Israel and, through Israel, all men. This last narrative is the story of Ruth in the book of the same name.

The narrative begins with famine and death. Throughout the Old Testament, natural catastrophes are used of Yahweh as a means of discipline to draw His people back to Himself and to demonstrate His power. The book of Judges focuses on Yahweh's use of other nations as His rod of discipline, but Ruth opens with "famine in the land." As a result of the famine, Elimelech, with his wife and two sons, forsook their inheritance in Bethlehem to live in the land of Moab where Elimelech and his two sons died. Prior to their death, the sons had married Moabite women. Naomi, Elimelech's wife, having heard that Yahweh had given bread to His people, determined to return to her home in Bethlehem. The two Moabite women started out with her, but only one, Ruth, continued to Bethlehem. The narrative continues to the end culminating in the genealogy to David from Perez, the firstborn of Judah and Tamar.

Once again Yahweh is demonstrating His oversight and faithfulness. Judah had five sons. His first two, Er and Onan, were wicked and Yahweh killed them. His third son was Shelah. These three sons were children of Judah and a Canaanite woman, the daughter of Shua. His fourth and fifth sons were the illegitimate offspring of Judah and Tamar, Judah's daughter-in-law. Judah's first three sons, being the sons of a Canaanite woman, would be problematic as the fathers of the Tribe of Judah. The illegitimacy of Perez and Zerah placed the constraints of the Law on the sons of Judah. "One of illegitimate birth shall not enter the assembly of Yahweh; even to the tenth generation none of his descendants shall enter the assembly of Yahweh."[348]

The last word in the Book of Ruth is David. David is the first King of Judean descent. David is the King with whom Yahweh makes a Covenant: "...and your kingdom shall be established forever before you. Your throne shall be established forever."[349] Thus the Covenant God, Yahweh, even in the dark days of the Judges, prepares for the one to come as son of David. This one to come, Immanuel, fulfills the Abrahamic Covenant, Sinaitic Covenant, and the Davidic Covenant.

Ask Yourself...

- *Do I see evidence of God's faithfulness in my "dark days"?*
- *How has God brought blessing out of sin/sorrow/pain in my life?*

Here are some action steps you can start with today.

- List three promises of God that have sustained you through your "dark days."

Conclusion

FINAL WORD

Because you have kept My command to persevere, I also will keep you from the hour of trial which shall come upon the whole world, to test those who dwell on the earth. Behold, I am coming quickly! Hold fast what you have, that no one may take your crown. He who overcomes, I will make him a pillar in the temple of My God, and he shall go out no more. And I will write on him the name of My God and the name of the city of My God, the New Jerusalem, which comes down out of heaven from My God. And I will write on him My new name. (Revelation 3:10-12)

Yahweh, the Covenant God, figures prominently throughout the Book of Judges. He is the one who raises up deliverers. He is also faithful to the Covenant as the Israelites are oppressed for a consequence of breaking the Covenant was oppression by other nations. Yahweh's faithfulness is juxtaposed against man's unfaithfulness and weakness. Let us take a closer look at some of those who appear in the record of Judges.

Five characters from the Judge Era are listed in the "Heroes of Faith" chapter, Hebrews 11. Hebrews 11: 1 states, "Faith is the substance of things hoped for, the evidence of things not seen." We are also reminded that, "without faith it is impossible to please Him, for he who comes to God must believe that He is, and that He is a rewarder of those who diligently seek Him." The writer then proceeds to tell of specific instances of Old Testament faithfulness. Nearly all of these instances are from Genesis and Exodus. The writer then lists others who are examples of faithfulness without specifying the instance of faith. Let us meditate on the record and see if we can identify the faith of: Gideon, Barak, Samson, Jephthah, and Samuel. Before we begin let us note that the narratives in Judges that pertain to Gideon, Barak, Samson, and Jephthah are half of the book. The Samson narrative is the longest of the Judges and Gideon's is but slightly less (both being about one sixth of the Book of Judges). Why are these listed in Hebrews 11, and where is the evidence of their faith? What does their inclusion teach us regarding Faith?

Gideon, a skeptic weak in faith, is an example of one who has faith the size of a mustard seed. He asked for three signs to address his doubts. His faith being weak, Yahweh graciously gave him a fourth sign. The victory won over the Midianites could only be attributed to Yahweh. Such a victory became a "benchmark" for the Psalmist and Isaiah. His obedience that led to the great victory over Midian is "enough" to place him with the "Heroes of Faith."

What is God communicating by listing Barak among the "Heroes of Faith" and leaving Deborah off the list? Once again one who is weak in faith is listed among the faithful. His weakness is manifested in his unwillingness to go to war without Deborah. As a result of his weakness, Barak gets not the glory of victory because a woman, Jael, kills Sisera. Nevertheless there is evidence that Barak had faith. What is that evidence? His obedience to the command to engage with only his ten thousand men against the nine hundred chariots and Sisera's multitude is the evidence of Barak's faith. His obedience was honored by Yahweh as Yahweh fought on Israel's behalf via a storm. The chariots became mired in mud causing Sisera to flee on foot. Thus the song of the redeemed acknowledged Barak: "Arise, Barak, and lead your captives away and as Issachar, so was Barak sent into the valley under his command."

How can Samson be listed in Hebrews 11? When you think of Samson, do you think of him as a model of faith? How can this be? Did not Samson violate his Nazarite vow? Do we not think of Samson as a womanizer who disregards Yahweh's instructions to marry within Israel? What is the evidence of Samson's faith? Samson's confession to Delilah, "No razor has ever come upon my head, for I have been a Nazarite to God from my mother's womb. If I am shaven, then my strength will leave me, and I shall become weak, and be like any other man." It reveals his understanding of his consecration to God. His understanding was incomplete as demonstrated by the phrase, "he did not know that Yahweh had departed from him." Nevertheless, he knew that his consecration to Yahweh at birth set him apart to serve. Twice Samson calls upon Yahweh revealing a measure of faith. After his victory at Lehi, Samson becomes thirsty and acknowledges that the victory was Yahweh's and that he is Yahweh's servant. At the end of his life, Samson called upon Yahweh once again. Yahweh answers his prayer and Samson gives his life for the Sons of Israel. Faith may be dim, but dim faith is faith nevertheless.

Jephthah is the last character mentioned in Hebrews 11 from the Book of Judges. Once again we are confronted by the question, Where is the evidence of his faith? Again we must keep in mind that faith is evidenced by obedience. Jephthah's victory over Ammon and the fulfillment of his vow are evidence of faith. His faithfulness to his vow, as painful as it was, demonstrates a level of faith and trust that usually eludes us. How often do we fail to fulfill a promise due to inconvenience or the hasty nature of our promise? Which is better, to be remembered for your faith or reneging on your vow to save your daughter?

The Judge Era closes with Samuel's anointing Saul as king. The previous four characters from the Judge Era would probably not be on our list of "Heroes of Faith" whereas Samuel probably would be. Samuel is one of the people in the Old Testament that mark a turning point in the life of Israel. He is the last judge and the first prophet in the new theocratic order. Samuel's life is characterized by faith from his first hearing of Yahweh's voice until his death. Yahweh used Samuel to: anoint Saul and David, confront the sin of Saul, the sin of the Sons of Israel, and Yahweh's hand was against the Philistines all the days of Samuel. Samuel's tenure as judge / prophet became a "benchmark" for Passover observance.

> *There had been no Passover kept in Israel like that since the days of Samuel the prophet and none of the kings of Israel had kept such a Passover as Josiah kept, with the priests and the Levites, all Judah and Israel who were present, and the inhabitants of Jerusalem. (2 Chronicles 35:18)*

Samuel's tenure as prophet/judge is exemplary, but his faith was not different than the faith of Samson, Gideon, Jephthah, and Barak. Samuel's faith may have been stronger, but not different.

Dear reader, the God revealed in the pages of Judges is the same God we serve. Both the Abrahamic Covenant and Siniaitic Covenant are fulfilled in and through Jesus, Immanuel. Throughout the Book of Judges the Covenant God intervened in the life of His people disciplining them, calling them back to Himself, and sustaining them. Each of the interventions foreshadows the ultimate intervention of the "Word made Flesh." The ultimate intervention was of a deliverer who delivers from sin, death, and gives life eternal.

Consequently we have hope for the life to come and all that the new heaven and new earth hold for us. We also have the privilege of being a chosen generation, a royal priesthood, a holy nation, His own special people. Therefore let us serve Him with gladness as we proclaim the praises of Him who called us out of darkness into His marvelous light.[350]

Lastly, Judges is the record of Yahweh's grace as He molds sinners such as Gideon, Jephthah, Samson, and Barak into "Heroes of Faith." In like manner He chose an idolater, Aaron, as the high priest and transformed him to "glory and beauty."[351] This shows the great grace of God in transforming sinners into vessels of honor for His people and the advancement of His name in the world.

Here are some action steps you can start with today.

- Which portion(s) of Judges were most useful to you in speaking of Jesus? Write them down.
- Which portion(s) of Judges were most hopeful? Write them down.

This book does not exhaust what the Book of Judges has to teach of Jesus or to give hope. But hopefully it will help you to read the whole of the Old Testament so that you will learn to see how the Old Testament testifies of Jesus and gives hope. Write down a plan to read the Old Testament.

Yahweh bless you and keep you;
Yahweh make His face shine upon you,
And be gracious to you;
Yahweh lift up His countenance upon you,
And give you peace.
(Numbers 6: 24 - 26)

ENDNOTES

1 John 5: 31 - 47

2 Luke 24:13-27

3 Luke 24:44-49

4 Romans 15:4

5 Romans 4:23

6 http://amazingsalvation.blogspot.com/2011/02/ben-hooper-story-whos-your-daddy.html

7 Joshua 9

8 Genesis 15

9 Exodus 3

10 Exodus 3:15

11 Exodus 19:5-6

12 Psalm 95; 96; 97; 135; Exodus 18:11

13 Psalm 47:2; 95:3; Malachi 1:14

14 Exodus 4:11; 1 Samuel 2:6-8; Jeremiah 10:16

15 Exodus 15; Psalm 70

16 Matthew 5:17

17 Matthew 22:37-40

18 1 Peter 2:9-10

19 Exodus 24:12; 31:18

20 Exodus 32:1-6

21 Exodus 20:3

22 Exodus 32:19

23 Exodus 32:7-9

24 Exodus 32: 11 – 14, 30 - 32

25 Exodus 34: 10 - 27

26 Deuteronomy 31-Joshua 1

27 Joshua 23, 24

28 1 Samuel 11:14- 12:25

29 Joshua 24:14

30 Joshua 24:6-13

31 Joshua 24:19-27

32 1 Samuel 11:14-12:1

33 1 Samuel 8:5

34 1 Samuel 8:7-8; 12:17

35 1 Samuel 12:6-12

36 Exodus 23:22

37 Deuteronomy 20:1-4

38 I Samuel 8:9

39 I Samuel 12:13–15

40 1 Samuel 12:23

41 Acts 3:24

42 Numbers 33: 51 - 56

43 Proverbs 16: 9

44 Exodus 3-4

45 Deuteronomy 31:7-8, 23; Joshua 1:1-9

46 Exodus 2:1ff

47 Numbers 13:8; Isaiah 11:13

48 Genesis 49:22-26

49 Joshua 17:14-18

50 Genesis 48:13 -20

51   note particularly Hosea 5:5-15; Isaiah 7:17

52   Exodus 3

53   Exodus 20:1-2

54   Genesis 35: 21 – 26; 49, 3,4

55   Genesis 34; 49:5-7

56   Genesis 2:25-26; Matthew 19:4-5

57   Genesis 31: 19, 33-35; 35: 1- 7

58   Judges 1:2

59   Judges 2:10-16

60   Numbers 14:24

61   Numbers 14:24

62   www.Familylife.com

63   Judges 2: 14b

64   Judges 2: 21-22; 3:1, 2

65   Exodus 12:35-36

66   Exodus 16:1-7, 31-36; Deuteronomy 8; Joshua 5:12; Exodus 15: 22-
     27; 17:1-7; Numbers 20:8-13

67   Exodus 14:13ff

68   Numbers 21

69   Judges 2:10b

70   Genesis 3:15

71   Matthew 5:17-20

72   Judges 2:17

73   Jeremiah 7:25

74   Deuteronomy 5:24-27; Exodus 20:18-21

75   Exodus 7:1

76   Amos 8:11-14; Ezekiel 20:3, 31

77   Deuteronomy 18:14-22

78   Jeremiah 23:13-32

[79] Exodus 3:10-17

[80] I Samuel 3:1-21

[81] I Kings 19: 15 – 21; II Kings 2: 7 – II Kings 13

[82] Isaiah 6:1-13

[83] Jeremiah 1:1-19

[84] Jeremiah 1:18

[85] Ezekiel 1-3:10

[86] Ezekiel 10

[87] Jeremiah 32:1-5

[88] Ezekiel 10-11:25

[89] Jeremiah 20:7

[90] Amos 3:8

[91] Jeremiah 5:31

[92] Jeremiah 14:13

[93] Deuteronomy 18:21-22

[94] Jeremiah 28:1-17

[95] Deuteronomy 13:1-5

[96] Deuteronomy 23:5

[97] II Peter 2:15; Jude 11

[98] 1 Samuel 2:27-36; I Kings 12:22-24; 13:1-10; 22:8-28; 2 Chronicles 15:1-8

[99] Matthew 22:37 and Deuteronomy 6:5

[100] Matthew 22:39 and Lev. 19:18

[101] 1 Samuel 15:22, 23; Isaiah 1:10-17; Jeremiah 7:23, 24; Hosea 6:6

[102] Jeremiah 31:27-34

[103] Ezekiel 18:4-32

[104] Jeremiah 23:22; Zechariah 1:4

[105] Judges 2:18

[106] Judges 2:16, 18

107 Judges 2:1

108 Ruth 2:4

109 Judges 6:27

110 Judges 8:18

111 Exodus 3:12

112 Joshua 1:5

113 Leviticus 2:11

114 Judges 6:36-40

115 Judges 7:7-14

116 Luke 1:5-23

117 Luke 1:26-38

118 Genesis 11:30; 18:10-15

119 1 Samuel 1:2-18

120 Luke 1:7-25

121 Numbers 6:2-21

122 I Samuel 1:9; 4:18

123 Genesis 22:11

124 Genesis 46:2

125 Exodus 3:4

126 Judges 8:28

127 Judges 8:1-21

128 Judges 6:25-32

129 Judges 8:24-27

130 1 Samuel 3:19-4:18

131 1 Samuel 7:1-17

132 Acts 13:20

133 Acts 3:24

134 1 Samuel 9:15-27; 10:17-27; 16:1-13

135 John 8:21-30

[136] Numbers 11:29

[137] Jude 1:1; 1 Peter 1:15; 2:9; 2 Peter 1:3

[138] Exodus 3:12

[139] Joshua 1:5

[140] Exodus 3:10

[141] Judges 2:16, 18

[142] Exodus 15:2, 2 Samuel 22:50, 51; Psalm 68:19, 20; Jeremiah 3:21-25

[143] Judges 3:10

[144] Judges 6:34

[145] Judges 11:29

[146] Judges 14:6, 19; 15:14

[147] Judges 16:20

[148] Matthew 4:1; Mark 1:12, 13; Luke 4:1ff

[149] Hebrews 2:14-15

[150] Luke 4:14

[151] Luke 4:18-19; Isaiah 61:1-2

[152] Matthew 12:18-21

[153] John 3:31-36

[154] Acts 1:1-3

[155] Acts 2

[156] John 14-16

[157] 1 Peter 4:10-11

[158] Judges 3:9-11

[159] Numbers 14:24

[160] Joshua 14:6-15

[161] Joshua 15:16, 17; Judges 1:12, 13

[162] Judges 1:19, 21, 27-36

[163] Exodus 23:33

[164] Judges 3:5- 6

165 Judges 3:9-11

166 Exodus 19:5-6

167 Deuteronomy 17: 18

168 Judges 11:27

169 Judges 3: 9

170 1 Corinthians 11:1

171 John 13:13-14

172 John 13:34-35

173 1 Kings 17:10-24

174 2 Kings 8:8-15

175 Judges 3:28

176 Judges 3:15

177 Deuteronomy 32:15-18; 1 Corinthians 10:20

178 Matthew 12:29; Hebrews 2:14-15

179 Judges 3:31

180 Judges 5:6

181 Luke 2:1

182 John 19:1-6, 19-22

183 Acts 11:28; 18:2; 25

184 Habakkuk 3: 18, 19

185 Deuteronomy 32:17

186 Judges 5:6-8

187 Judges 5:7

188 Exodus 18:13

189 1 Kings 10:23-25

190 Isaiah 2:2-4

191 Exod. 18:13, Judg. 4:4

192 Exod. 18:13, Judg. 4:5

193 Exod. 7:16, Judg. 4:6

[194] Deut. 18:15, Judg. 4:4

[195] Exod. 39:43, Judg. 5:24

[196] Deut. 27:15, Judg. 5:23

[197] Joshua, Barak

[198] Exod. 14:14, Judg. 4:6

[199] Exod. 14:24, Judg. 4:15

[200] Exod. 14, Judg. 4

[201] Exod. 15, Judg. 5

[202] Exod. 15:1

[203] Judg. 5:1

[204] Acts 3:22-23; Matthew 16:13-14; 21:11, 46; Mark 6:15; Luke 7:16; 24:19

[205] Numbers 12:1- 8

[206] vs. 6, 7

[207] vs. 9

[208] vs. 14

[209] Acts 21: 7 - 11

[210] Revelation 2:20

[211] 1 Kings 10:23-25

[212] Judges 5:6-7)

[213] Judges 5:7

[214] Judges 5:12-18

[215] Judges 5:3-5, 9, 23, 31

[216] Numbers 11:29

[217] Numbers 1:2-3;14:28-29

[218] Judges 6:25-32

[219] Deuteronomy 7:5

[220] Judges 6:36-40

[221] Judges 7:1-8

[222] Judges 7:22

[223] Judges 8:13-17

[224] Judges 5

[225] Judges 5:15b-17

[226] Judges 8:22-23

[227] Judges 8:24-27

[228] Judges 6:14

[229] Judges 6:34

[230] Judges 7

[231] Judges 8:22-23

[232] Judges 8:28

[233] Hebrews 11:32

[234] Psalm 83:9

[235] Isaiah 9:4ff

[236] Judges 10:14

[237] Judges 9:6

[238] Judges 9:23, 56, 57

[239] Judges 9:1-6

[240] Judges 9:23-56

[241] Judges 9:23-25

[242] Judges 9:57

[243] Judges 9:7-21

[244] Judges 9, 15, 16, 19-21

[245] Genesis 12:6-7

[246] Genesis 33:18-20

[247] Genesis 35:1-4

[248] Joshua 8:30-35;24

[249] Exodus 20: 25; Deuteronomy 27: 5

[250] Joshua 8:32-35

251 Joshua 24

252 Joshua 24:14-28

253 Joshua 20:7-9

254 Joshua 21:20-21

255 Amos 5:21-24

256 Jeremiah 2:29-37

257 Deuteronomy 11:29

258 Judges 9:19

259 Judges 9:23, 56-57

260 Judges 10:13

261 Hebrews 12:5-6

262 Judges 11:1-10

263 Judges 11:10-11

264 Judges 11:12-28

265 Judges 11:29

266 Judges 11:32-33

267 Judges 11:30-40

268 Judges 10:13

269 Judges 10:7

270 2 Samuel 8:1

271 Exodus 24:7; see also Exodus 24:3

272 Psalm 31:5

273 Matt. 5:37

274 Exodus 34:13-16; Deuteronomy 7:3-4; Joshua 23:12; Judges 3:5-6

275 Judges 10:1-5; 12:8-15

276 Judges 2:18

277 Judges 1:1

278 Judges 21:25

279 Judges 2:11-23

[280] Judges 18:20

[281] Lamentations 3:21-24

[282] Genesis 8:21-22; 9:9-17

[283] Psalm 118

[284] Judges 15:11

[285] Judges 14:1-4

[286] Judges 14:6, 19; 15:14

[287] Judges 16

[288] Judges 15:18-20

[289] Judges 13:5

[290] Judges 2:16

[291] Judges 16:15-19

[292] Judges 16:28

[293] Deuteronomy 20:1-4; Exodus 14:13-14; Isaiah 30:1-3; Exodus 34:10-17; 2 Chronicles 20:35-37; Psalm 118:5-9

[294] Exodus 17: 1- 7; Numbers 20: 2- 13

[295] 1 Samuel 2:12-17, 22-25

[296] 1 Samuel 3:11-14

[297] Num. 4:1-3; 8:23-26

[298] 1 Samuel 3:11-14

[299] 1 Samuel 4:13

[300] Titus 2:2

[301] 1 Samuel 3:16-18

[302] 1 Samuel 3:19-20

[303] Acts 3:24; 13: 20

[304] 1 Samuel 13:11-14; 15:10-31

[305] 1 Samuel 16:1-13

[306] 1 Samuel 7:1-14

[307] I Samuel 7:10

[308] 1 Samuel 7:9-10

[309] Exodus 17:8-16

[310] 1 Samuel 7:15-17

[311] 1 Samuel 12:23

[312] 1 Samuel 8:7

[313] John 1:1, 5, 14

[314] Hebrews 1:1-2

[315] Hebrews 7-10

[316] Romans 8:34; 1 John 2:1

[317] Matthew 28:18; Isaiah 9:6-7; Revelation 5:11-14: 19:1-16; Matthew 2:1-2, 27:11

[318] 1 Peter 2:9

[319] Note the extensive instructions regarding the priests, their garments, and their duties in Exodus and Leviticus.

[320] Exodus 29:1

[321] Exodus 32:11-14, 30-35

[322] Joshua 13:14; Deuteronomy 18:1-8 also Numbers 18; Deuteronomy 10:8-9

[323] Numbers 35:2-8; Deuteronomy 14:27-29; 18:1-5

[324] 1 Samuel 8:1-22

[325] Judges 2:10-23

[326] Judges 20:28; Deuteronomy 10:8; 18:1-5; Joshua 24:33

[327] Exodus 28

[328] Exodus 28:40-43, 29:9; Leviticus 8

[329] Joshua 19:40-46

[330] Judges 1:34

[331] Joshua 19: 47 – 48; Judges 18

[332] Joshua 18:1; 1 Samuel 1:3, 4:3-4

[333] Judges 18:30; 2 Kings 10:29, 17:6; Amos 8:11-14

[334] Exodus 32:27-28

[335] Romans 2:4

[336] 2 Peter 3:15

[337] 2 Peter 2:15; Jude 1:11

[338] Genesis 38:24; Leviticus 21:9

[339] Ezekiel 16

[340] Proverbs 18:9

[341] See Matthew 27:3-5

[342] see Matthew 26:75; Mark 14:72; Luke 22:60-62; John 21:15-19

[343] Hebrews 7-8; Romans 8:34

[344] Hebrews 9:16-10:18; 1 John 1:7-2:2

[345] Ephesians 2:14-18

[346] Romans 5:1

[347] Colossians 3:15; Philippians 4:7

[348] Genesis 38; Deuteronomy 23:2

[349] 2 Samuel 7:16

[350] 1 Peter 2:9

[351] Ex.28:2, 40

CPSIA information can be obtained at www.ICGtesting.com
Printed in the USA
BVOW02s0240220514

354189BV00002B/5/P